for Muslims, Christians, Jews,
and all seekers of knowledge

Remember Who You Are

28 Spiritual Verses
from the Holy Quran
to Help You Discover
Your True Identity, Purpose,
and Nourishment in God

Rahim Snow

REMEMBRANCE STUDIO

Published by Remembrance Studio

Edited by Jennifer Snow

Book design by Rahim Snow

This book is typeset in Feijoa, designed by Kris Sowersby, and
FF Milo, designed by Michael Abbink and Paul van der Laan.
The book cover is typeset in FF Milo Serif, also designed by
Michael Abbink.

Special thanks to Rebecca Foote and the Nasser D. Khalili
Collection of Islamic Art for supporting me in using the Cal-
ligraphic Lion of Ahmed Hilmi (cal 242) in their collection to
derive the lion outline on the book cover.

Remember Who You Are / Rahim Snow. — 1st ed.

ISBN 978-0-9988262-0-2

RS1.1.0.0

Join my mailing list at

http://join.rahimsnow.com

to read other writings

and get sneak peeks into future books.

Dedicated

to my beloved son and daughter

Khalil and Maya

with love and amazement

Contents

Now, Serve

Epilogue

Artist's Prayer

In the name of Allah,
Being of all beings,
Artist of all artists,
Teacher of all teachers,
Lord of all the worlds,
The Caring, the Compassionate,
God above all else,
Friend like no other—
I offer this humble work
In service, friendship, and love for you,
And I ask in the names
Of the high ambassadors of God—
Muhammad and Ali, Mary and Fatima,
Moses and Shekinah, Jesus and the Holy Spirit,
Peace be upon them all—
That this work may help the people of God
Remember that they are the people of God—
Yet only with your will and blessing upon it.
Thank you, Allah, for making me
What you have made me.
Thank you, Allah, for giving me
What you have given me.
Thank you, Allah, for helping me to give
What you have given me to give.
All greatness, all glory, and all praise belong to you.
Here I am, Allah,
At your service,
Here I am.

Acknowledgements

First, I am thankful to Allah, without whom I would not be. Thank you, Allah, for creating me. Thank you for raining your blessings and gifts down on me. Thank you for entrusting the task of writing this particular book to me. Thank you for helping me to fulfill that trust. It has been an honor and an adventure to serve you and work with you on this book. What would you like me to work on next? Here I am, Allah; at your service, here I am.

Second, I am thankful to my mother and father, Kulsoom and Liaquatali, without whom I would not have been born or been born a Muslim. Their interest in spiritual practice, religious studies, and interfaith dialogue formed the foundations of my own interest. It was my mother's love for religious stories and my father's love for religious philosophy that nourished my imagination and led it inward and upward. I love you both very much. Thank you for letting your spirituality be a beautiful starting point for my own.

Third, I am thankful to my wife, Jennifer. You would not be holding this book in your hands if it wasn't for her unwavering support. She didn't just encourage me to write it. She insisted that it must be written and that

I must be the one to write it. Through all the ups and downs of life and the storms of doubt, she believed in me. For that, I love you and thank you from the bottom of my heart.

Fourth, I am thankful to all my friends and mentors who have helped me, taught me, changed me, encouraged me, and have been interested in what I was doing. Every little bit has helped me get to this point.

Snowball and Snowflake (my beloved cats)
Nuri Daya
Barbara Graham
Riaz Virji
Michael Wolenetz
R. D. Sharif
Shiraz Kabani
Shams Bhaloo
Mary Axford
David Morgen
Stevie Liang
Alondo Brewington

Fifth, I am thankful to all the teachers who were kind enough to teach me, to send their words out into the world, so they would reach the hungry imagination of a young Muslim boy in Atlanta. There are too many to name, but a few of them are:

Aga Khan III, Sir Sultan Muhammad Shah
Joseph Campbell
Jalal al-Din Rumi
Muhiyiddin Ibn al-Arabi

Henry Corbin
Muhammad Iqbal
Marianne Williamson
Clarissa Pinkola Estés
Robert Bly
Oprah Winfrey
Louis Massignon
Thomas Moore
Pema Chödrön
Mohammed Arkoun
Neguin Yavari
Sonia S'hiri
Keith Ward

To all of them and to all the unseen companions, angels, saints, and prophets who sent me their blessings to stay on my path and finish this book, I say with hands joined together: thank you, thank you, thank you to each and every one of you.

Finally, I am thankful to my teacher, His Highness the Aga Khan IV. When I was a young man, I used to read all your speeches in search of hidden treasures. Two passages from two different speeches stood out for me:

> As the demands on his time increase, every Muslim will find it more and more difficult to seek for himself the answer to the fundamental question of how he should live his life for it to be truly Muslim. It is men such as you who will have to bring forth the answers. Answers which will have to be practical and realistic in the world of today and tomorrow. (1976)

> What the Muslim world needs today, I suggest, is more of those innovative architects that can navigate between the twin dangers of slavishly copying the architecture of the past and of foolishly ignoring its rich legacy. It needs those who can thoroughly internalize the collective wisdom of bygone generations, the eternal Message and ethic with which we live, and then reinforce them in the language of tomorrow. (1989)

When I read those words, I knew I wanted to be a part of this movement and to make contributions toward this effort. I wanted to dig deep into the wisdom of Islam and bring forth practical answers in the language of tomorrow. This inspired me to continue my lifelong studies into religion, spirituality, mythology, and psychology.

After I finished college, you supported me in studying Islamic Studies and Humanities at the Institute of Ismaili Studies in London. And then you continued to support me as I got my Master's degree in Religion from the University of Oxford. Even more years would still have to pass before I could thoroughly internalize and integrate everything I had learned.

I am happy to report, dear teacher, that this book, *Remember Who You Are*, is the first fruit of the seed you planted in me years ago. And there is so much more to come, inshallah.

Thank you for everything you have done for me. Thank you for your leadership, your teachings, your guidance, your patronage, and your loving blessings. You have made a profound difference in my life. May the peace and blessings of God be upon the Prophet Muhammad and his family.

What Is This Book About?

1

You are a being from God.
You are good and beautiful.
You are forever.
Remember who you are.

2

Remember Who You Are is a practical handbook of spiritual teachings based on 28 core verses from the Quran.

Each verse is translated into simple readable English and accompanied by a teaching / reflection / commentary / examples that show you how to apply that verse in your daily life.

These core verses represent the essential ideas of a universal spirituality. Muslims, Christians, Jews, and all seekers of knowledge can use them to go deeper into their own practice.

3

This is the book I always wanted to read and carry around with me while I was a teenager, a college student, and a young man trying to figure out how to be a good Muslim, a good human being, who lives in a multicultural, multilingual, multiracial, and multifaith world.

I wanted a book to teach me the core truths of my life, give me space to raise questions, give me ideas, offer support, encouragement, and inspiration. But no such book was available.

No one was writing the kind of books I wanted to read. So I had to write one myself.

In this book, I explore the following questions:

1. How do I properly identify who and what I am?

2. How do I find my purpose? Why am I here? What am I supposed to be doing? What does a good meaningful life look like?

3. What is my proper food? What actually feeds me, nourishes me, heals me, makes me stronger?

4. How do I accept myself and learn to appreciate what God made when he made me? How do I stop criticizing and despising myself? How do I come out of hiding and show up? How do I break my silence and find my voice?

5. What do I have in common with all people? How can I appreciate all the differences among people? How do I find my tribe, my community, my circle? How do I stop feeling lonely?

6. How do I find God? How can I know God? How can I serve God? How do I build a down-to-earth relationship with God?

7. How do I respond to people who ignore / exclude / marginalize / undermine / hate / hurt others?

8. How do I discover my gifts and practice my art? How do I give what I was given to give? How do I create? How do I become part of the flow from God through me into the world (God → you → world)?

9. How do I overcome fear / cynicism / apathy / numbness / existential fatigue / paralysis so that I can show up / speak up / get my hands dirty / intervene / contribute / make a difference in the world? How can I help? How can I serve? What can I actually do?

10. What truths can I live by? What are the truths that will be true 50,000 years from now because they were true 50,000 years ago? What are the truths that will be true now and in the life hereafter? What are the truths that are timeless?

On the one hand, I could spend an entire lifetime searching for the answers to these questions. On the other hand, every day I live on this earth requires that I have good answers to these questions so I can make my daily decisions on strong foundations.

How do I bridge this gap? I ask God himself to teach me. Out of his caring and compassionate nature, he gives me answers that are both tangible so I can make good decisions today as well as spacious so I can keep exploring them over a lifetime. And that is what has made this book possible.

Introduction: The Lion and the Sheep

My mother and father, Kulsoom and Liaquatali, were my first spiritual teachers in life. Many people taught me about religion, but my parents were the ones who taught me about the spirituality inside religion—and they still do. One of the stories they used to tell me was the story of the lion and the sheep.

Once upon a time, there was a pregnant lioness who died giving birth to her baby lion. A flock of sheep came by and found the newborn lion, helpless and unable to care for himself. So they adopted the baby lion and made him a part of their flock.

Over the next many years, they raised him as if he was one of their own. So even though the baby lion grew bigger and much stronger than any sheep, he still walked like a sheep, played like a sheep, ate like a sheep, and made "ba-a-a-a" sounds like a sheep. They lived together like this for so long that everyone forgot that he was actually a lion, including the lion himself. He was more of a sheep-lion rather than a real lion. He was satisfied with his life as a sheep, but he was not particularly happy.

One day, all the sheep, including this sheep-lion, were eating grass together and playing sheep games. Suddenly an older lion jumped out of the bushes and charged toward them. All the sheep feared for their lives and ran away as fast as they could. The sheep-lion stood still and looked curiously at this older lion, who walked toward him like a king. Having lived with the sheep for so long, he had never seen such a royal creature before.

The older lion roared at the sheep-lion, almost as if to say, "What is a lion doing living like a sheep?" The sheep-lion had never heard such a sound. It was so powerful and scary at the same time. He didn't know what to do so he too ran away as fast as he could, following the tracks of his sheep friends.

He soon found them drinking water near a river. As he leaned down to join them, he saw the reflections of their faces in the water in comparison to his own face. All the sheep looked like each other, but he didn't look like any of them. He actually looked like that older kingly lion.

For the first time, he realized that he was different from all the other sheep. Seeing that kingly lion and hearing that kingly roar had stirred something in his heart that he could not ignore. He got a glimpse that there was something more to who he was and the life he was living. He knew then that he could no longer live with the sheep while pretending to be a sheep. So the next morning, in the hours before sunrise, he left his sheep friends as they slept to find other lions like himself.

He wanted to find out who he really was. He wanted to discover his true identity.

The Meaning Behind the Story

My mother didn't just tell me this story as a children's story and leave it at that. She said that there was a very important meaning behind it. She explained that this story is really our story, the story of all human beings. Like the lion who thinks he's a sheep, we are all beings from God who think we are physical bodies. We don't know who we really are, why we are here, or what our proper food is. Eating, playing, and sleeping, we live like sheep without being aware of our true nature. My mother explained that this is why God sent down the scriptures and the prophets. He wanted to reverse this tendency to forget so we can remember and rediscover our spiritual nature.

Though my mother told me different parts of this story throughout my childhood and teenage years, it was only many years later that I put all the pieces together and tried to go deeper into the meaning. While studying the symbolism of religious stories, I discovered that this story of the lion and the sheep was very old. It comes in many versions and can be found across India, other parts of Asia, and the Middle East. But the point of the story was the same everywhere: we have forgotten who we are.

That's a good start, I used to ask myself, but what's the next step? The story says the lion goes in search of other lions. And then what? How does he actually rediscover who he is? It's not enough for us to know the story and understand its meaning. We want to use the meaning to fulfill the real point of the story: to free the lion inside us all. We don't just want storytelling and symbolism; we want transformation. In other words, how do we fulfill the meaning behind this story in our very own lives so that we can become fully aware of who we really are and live from that core?

I have searched long and hard for the answer to that question and this is what I've found so far. As beings from God, we have the nature of a lion. Our minds and hearts, however, have been educated to act like sheep. We are all courageous and powerful at our core, but we make decisions out of the fear and helplessness in our minds and hearts. Courage and fear don't match. Power and helplessness don't match. And as long as there's a mismatch, we suffer from confusion and unhappiness.

Even though we can force ourselves to live like sheep and accept this as our lot in life, something in our minds and hearts remains restless. Many of us suffer from fears, doubts, anxieties, depression, apathy, cynicism, and powerlessness. These are the painful symptoms that come up when we forget our true identity, stay unaware of our true purpose, and never receive our true nourishment.

The bad news is that this case of mistaken identity can last a very long time. Why? Because to be confused about your identity is not as painful as putting your hand in fire. If you accidentally put your hand in fire, the pain is so immediate and so severe that you will instinctively pull your hand back out and begin to nurse it and massage it and find a way to soothe the burning. But what if there was no pain when you put your hand in fire? What if, instead, you had a mild sense of discomfort, distraction, loss, sadness, and uncertainty? That's not much of a signal to tell you to get your hand out of the fire right now. In a few minutes, the fire would have consumed your hand.

Our mistaken identity is the same way. It's not severely painful, so we accept it and find temporary relief through a variety of entertaining and soothing distractions. But the mistaken identity remains intact and offers us the anxious little life of a sheep with all its creature comforts and complaints while quietly robbing us of that larger life of a lion that we were meant to live and in which we find our true identity and purpose and nourishment in God.

The good news is that the spell of this mistaken identity can be broken. The best way to do that is to learn from those who have already broken the spell and remembered who they really are. In the same way that we once learned how to live like sheep from other sheep, we now have to unlearn all that and re-learn how to live like lions from other lions. Living in a community of sheep will never introduce us to our proper nature as lions. Only by learning from other lions, practicing what they teach us, and living in a community of like-minded lions can we rediscover our true identity.

In the same way that our sheep education was holding us back, our lion education can free us to move forward. Once our minds and hearts begin to act like the lions we are at our core, all the confusion and unhappiness that comes from having a mistaken identity are eliminated. That is when we can have our true joy and courage and strength and creativity restored to us.

A Few Good Lions
So where do we find a few good lions who are willing to teach us? For the people of God, three of our greatest lions are Muhammad, Jesus, and Moses (peace be upon them all). And the point of all the messages they

have brought to us from God is this: wake up from your forgetfulness and remember who you are. You are not scared little sheep who can be satisfied with grazing on a little patch of grass. You are powerful lions who are capable of accomplishing amazing things in the name of God.

In other words, you are not fragile mortal bodies living on the earth for a few years, waiting for your turn to die, hoping to get into heaven. You are ever-living beings who come from the ever-living God to work his will and serve as his ambassadors and artists on earth. The true purpose of religion is to help us remember who we are and reawaken the lion in us; everything else is the sleep of the sheep.

Now living for years as sheep does not mean that we are going to snap our fingers and fully restore the lion in us overnight. We are not going to embrace our lion nature so intensely and quickly that we suddenly erase all the years of conditioning we've received to make us act like sheep. We need a period of unlearning and re-learning. We need a period of education and transition. We need models, we need community, we need reminders, and we need practices. We need space to experiment, room to grow, choices to go down different roads, and opportunities to get creative. We need allowances to make mistakes, to learn from our mistakes, and to get back on track. Above all else, we need God's grace to hold in our minds and hearts a larger vision of our lives and the courage to pursue it.

God already knows we need a lot of support and he has always been working to provide it. When his kindness overflowed for the early Jewish community, he gave them Moses as a model and the Torah as a reminder. Centuries later, when his kindness overflowed for the early Christian community, he gave them Jesus as a model and the Gospel as a reminder. Again centuries later, when his kindness overflowed for the early Muslim community, he gave them Muhammad as a model and the Quran as a reminder. If we compare all three models and all three reminders, we will begin to see patterns and practices that God has been using for thousands of years to help us remember who we are.

Where This Book Fits In

Given this rich history of God's grace, what I want to do in this book is to focus on the Quran as a powerful reminder of who we really are. This is not a comprehensive study of the Quran, of course. This is an introduction to 28 core verses that help you discover your true identity, purpose, and nourishment in God. Each verse is translated into simple readable English and accompanied by a teaching / reflection / commentary / examples to help us apply that verse in our daily lives.

In addition to helping us remember who we are, this book of is also helpful in other ways. For example, as a teenager I often wished someone would write a book about the Quran in simple English that spoke to the Muslim experience of growing up in today's world. I wanted a book written in my own style of talking and thinking that helped me better understand the essential message of the Quran. That book never came out. I had to grow up without it and make my own way. As I wrote this book, I often found myself saying, "I really wish I could have read this book when I was a teenager." So for all the 21st century Muslims looking for a book written in a contemporary style that reinforces the essential message of the Quran and helps them remember what really matters, here's one book that might help.

In the same way, I am often surprised that Christians, Jews, and all seekers of knowledge don't have a good book on the Quran to help them grow stronger in their own practice. There are dated translations and commentaries of the Quran, there are academic books that talk about themes in the Quran, but there are no contemporary books that show you how to use the Quran to become stronger in your own faith without converting to Islam. So for all the Christians, Jews, and others interested in letting the Quran complement your own scriptures and be an additional source of nourishment for your own religious and spiritual lives, here's one book that might help.

Finally, there are many people who are simply curious to know more about the spirituality of Islam. They have a variety of historical, political, and poetic books to choose from, yet none of them go deeply into the verses of the Quran themselves. Picking up a translation of the entire Quran and trying to understand it yourself can be intimidating. Wouldn't it be helpful to get an introduction to a handful of core verses so that you get a friendly window into the essential message of the Quran? So for all the people who are simply curious to learn more about the spirituality of Islam, here's one book that might help.

It is my conviction that if you take these verses seriously and personally, if you study and apply the meaning of these verses in your daily life—no matter what religious background you come from—God's grace will elevate your life to a new level. Why? By putting in the time and effort to understand and practice the meaning of these verses, you are fulfilling the purpose for which God sent the prophets and the scriptures into the world. You are actively allowing and inviting God to take his proper place in your life. If you are doing the very thing he has asked you to do, how can he not do the very thing he has promised to do? So practice these verses and let God enlarge your life by helping you remember who you are.

Inshallah (as God wills).

How To Use This Book

1

You can read this book cover to cover or just open the book to any verse. You can also study one verse a day and repeat the process for the 28 days of the lunar month.

For example, on the first day of the month, start with the first verse. Read it in the morning. Think about it throughout the day. Try to apply it to your thoughts, to your emotions, to the events that are happening on that day. Before you go to sleep, review the same verse again and reflect on how you used the verse that day.

Ask yourself: "What did I learn? How did I feel? Did I get a different understanding of the verse? How did God use the events of my day to help me get a better understanding of this verse?"

On the second day, read the second verse, and so on, for 28 days. For the remaining days of the month, reflect on the 28 verses and pick a few that you would like to spend some more time with. When the next month starts, start over with the first verse. Repeat this practice of studying and applying a verse to your daily life as often as you can.

2

The translation of each verse and the accompanying teaching are my interpretations, based on my research, understanding, practice, and prayer. There are many other possible interpretations and I encourage you to study them all. I also encourage you to develop your own interpretations that will foster more goodness and beauty in the world. I offer mine simply as a starting point in your explorations.

The key to getting any real benefit from these verses is to spend time with them, reflect on them in a prayerful manner, and let them inspire your thoughts, your feelings, and your actions. Make an intention to go deeper into them every time you study them. Ask God to help you in this practice and then be willing to receive his help.

The ideas in this book are so essential to the subject of remembering who you are that they are repeated several times across different chapters. This repetition should not be regarded as unnecessary and tedious. The purpose of the repetition is to introduce the ideas to you multiple times and in multiple ways. Once you reflect on the core ideas deliberately and practice them daily, then you can begin to thoroughly internalize them and make them a core part of your life.

3

Allah is the Arabic word for God. God is Allah. Allah is God. There is no essential difference between these words. They are two names from two different languages that refer to the one Creator.

4

When I refer to God with the words "he" or "his" or "him," I don't capitalize them unless they occur at the beginning of a sentence. I keep them as lowercase words to create a sense of familiarity and intimacy with God. This is perfectly natural in the Quran because there are no uppercase or lowercase letters in Arabic. Also, in the language of Urdu, which is my mother tongue, God is addressed as "tu(n)" (informal you) and not "aap" (formal you). This is yet another example where informal language is used to create a friendly intimacy with God.

PROLOGUE

1

CHANGE YOUR INSIDES

*God doesn't change
what's happening in people's lives
until they first change
what's happening inside themselves.*

(Quran 13:11)

How many times have you tried to change something in your life and found that it's just not working? How long have you dreamed of having something in your life and found that it's just not coming? How hard have you struggled to get rid of something from your life and found that it's just not leaving?

For example, you might want to get a promotion, advance your career, or grow your business. You might want that one best friend or a wider circle of friends to go through the ups and downs of life with you. You might want to build a life with a partner, raise children, and travel the world with them. You might want to wear nicer clothes, live in a fancier home, and make more money. You might want to feel like you finally made it and that you are some-body in the world.

No matter what it is that you want—whether it's material, physical, emotional, intellectual, social, or financial—you believe that getting it is going to substantially change your life. You think it's going to give you more fulfillment than ever before. You think it's going to bring you more attention and respect. Most importantly, you think it's going to help you feel differently than how you're feeling right now.

At first, you try to make the change and get the thing you want all by yourself, but it often doesn't happen. Then you decide you might need God for this one, so you start praying. You start praying a lot. But it still doesn't happen. You wonder what you're doing wrong. You wonder why God is not giving you what you want. Is he not listening, you ask yourself? Does he not care? Other people al-ready have what you want, so when is it going to be your turn? You even start to wonder if something is deeply wrong with you.

Then one day it happens: you finally get what you want! It's so exciting—for a few minutes or a few days or a few months. Then the excitement fades. It doesn't change your life. It doesn't change your status in the world either. You might feel better for a little while, but then you go back to the usual feeling of dissatisfaction that you felt before. So you move on to the next thing on your list of wants. And you wonder if this new thing might be the one to make a real difference in your life. You wonder if this moment might be the one when God takes a decisive step to improve your life.

This game of wanting something, getting it, losing interest in it, and moving on to something else is not harmless. It is a vicious circle that lies to you about who you are, why you are here, and what feeds you. It wants you to believe that you are not enough and that everything you have is not enough. It wants you to stay preoccupied with what you don't have, so you can always stay busy chasing after it. It wants you to believe that you are stuck in a state of lack. Once you get hooked on these lies, you forget the truth of who you are. As a result, you can only think of yourself as a player trying to survive and win the game. This becomes your false identity, your false purpose, and your false nourishment.

This verse says that God doesn't change what's happening in our lives until we first change what's happening inside ourselves. On the outside, it looks like we are ambitious people going after what we want and eventually getting it. On the inside, however, we feel anxious, desperate, and lost. Ever since our minds and hearts began to focus on the lack, they have been trapped in a vicious circle of endless wanting. They have been playing this losing game out of a desperate attempt to overcome the lack.

The lack, however, is a lie. The game of wanting and getting is a lie. The vicious circle is a lie. God is not interested in keeping these lies going and having them occupy and dominate our insides. He wants us to work on changing our insides by learning to give up these lies and rediscover the truth. In other words, he wants us to remember who we are.

We are not creatures who lack things, but beings from God who arrive in the world with his blessings and gifts and favors without measure. This is our true identity. We find our fulfillment not by chasing and collecting things, but by serving God and sharing his blessings with all of creation. This is our true purpose. We receive our daily bread not from fame and fortune, but from our service and devotion to God. This is our true nourishment.

This remembrance of who we are, why we are here, and what feeds us reorients our minds and hearts toward God. God wants our minds to become students of his mind. That means we have to think about things the way he thinks about them. God wants our hearts to become friends of his heart. That means we have to care about things the way he cares about them. Instead of orienting our lives, our concerns, and our goals toward ourselves and our wants, we reorient them toward God and his wants. Instead of making ourselves the center of our lives, we make God the center of our lives. This is what changes our insides. And that is precisely what invites God to change our lives.

What does this actually look like? When you remember that you are a being from God who has come to the world for a noble purpose, then you can't help but to think about your list of wants differently. You don't have to chase all the things on that list anymore because you don't need them to give you your identity, purpose, and nourishment. You don't need to pursue them out of a sense of desperation and lack. You can revisit and revise each item on your list to make sure it serves what God wants.

You have often told God what you want, but have you ever asked God what he wants? Have you seen his wish list? Do you know what his goals are in making the world and putting people in it? Do you know what kind of cultures and civilizations he wants to see? Do you know what kind of person God wants you to be? He will teach you if you ask and listen and study and learn.

Then you can rewrite your list of wants by putting what God wants at the top. God certainly wants you to have all kinds of good and beautiful experiences in the world. But he doesn't want to limit them only to health, wealth, and family. He has made you for a much larger purpose in which all those things are included. When you adopt what God wants as your own wants and put them at the top of your list, he blesses and sanctifies your entire list. He multiplies and quickens the opportunities for all the experiences on your list to come into your life.

Now you can approach all the things on your list of wants from an attitude of service to God. Advancing your career or growing your business can help you serve your community more effectively. Cultivating friendships can help you appreciate our oneness and our differences. Building a life with a partner and raising a family can help you deepen your capacity for caring and compassion. Increasing your wealth can help you share even more with those who are in need. In this way, you can make serving God the primary intention and goal of all your efforts on earth.

So make what God wants your first priority. You can have ambitions for your life. You can stretch yourself to receive more of God's bounty. But be entirely devoted to God so that you give his ambitions more time, attention, and effort than your own. Pursue your dreams in the world, but let God help you be selective about which dreams to pursue. All dreams are not worthy of you. And you can go after them with enthusiasm, but reserve the best of your mind and heart for God. If you help God get what he wants, he will help you get what you want.

Work on changing your insides by learning that God will change your life when you remember who you are. When you reorient your mind and heart toward God, you will receive a sense of identity, purpose, and nourishment that you will never receive from playing the game of wanting and getting. In fact, when you remember that you are a being from God in the service of God, all kinds of blessings, gifts, and favors are given to you. Doors that would be closed are opened for you. Paths that would be covered with thorns are cleared for you. As you begin to change your insides, God begins to change your life. You gradually overcome the vicious circle of the game and live in the gracious spiral of God, drawing nearer and nearer to him, always and in all ways.

DECLARE

I am changing my insides.
God is changing my life.

FIRST, UNDERSTAND

2

YOU ARE A BEING FROM GOD

When he decides to bring something
into being, he says to it,
"Be" and it is.

(Quran 3:47)

The first step in remembering *who* you are is to recognize *what* you are, what you really are, and let that be the core of your identity.

What you really are has nothing to do with your name or nationality. It can't be defined by what you wear, what you look like, what you do, or what other people think of you. It also can't be defined by the roles you play in your family, community, workplace, or any other group. It goes much deeper.

If I ask you what you are, you might say, "I am a human being." You understand what it means to be a human, as opposed to being an animal or a plant or a rock. But what does it mean to be a being? What is the *being* of "human being"?

This verse says that when God decides to create something, he says to it "Be" and it is. By speaking the word "Be" (Arabic: *kun*) over it, God commands it to be, to be a being, to be real, to have life and will. You yourself were created in this way.

Once upon a time beyond time, God said the word "Be" and brought you into being. At first, he kept you to himself and you slept soundly like a hidden treasure in the privacy of his thoughts. He alone knew you. You were unknown to everyone else, unknown even to yourself. Then one day he began to wake you out of your sleep and speak to you and teach you. He no longer kept you hidden but revealed you to yourself and the rest of creation.

In this way, God made you a being from his own speaking. He didn't make you out of earth and water, like the way he made your body. He didn't make you out of more subtle elements, like the way he made your thoughts and emotions. He made you out of his own speech, his own voice, his own language.

That's why you are a being from God. You come directly from him. You don't come from anything in the heavens or the earth. You are a word from the mouth of God because he literally spoke you into being. And since the word he used to make you was

"Be", it affirms and confirms that what you are and what you have always been is a being. Give thanks to God for this.

Now keep in mind that this being that you are is not an abstract concept. It is not a symbol. It is not something you have to believe in. It is a fact. It is the fundamental fact that lives beneath all your experiences. Before you say or do anything, before you think or feel anything, first you must be. That is how fundamental being is to you and your life. You must first be in order to experience anything else.

This being that you are is the foundation for all that is true, good, and beautiful in you. It is your true nature as well as your true identity. The more you recognize it and get familiar with it, the more you can enjoy it and share all the blessings and gifts God put inside it. The more you identify with it and get centered in it, the more wisely and courageously you can meet every experience that comes your way.

So how do you recognize and identify with this being that you are? By understanding how being is different from experience and by learning to see that difference through practice. Being, by definition, always stays the same and never changes. Experience, on the other hand, never stays the same and keeps on changing. So you have to look and see what part of you stays the same and what part of you keeps changing. Let's practice some examples.

You say, "I am healthy" or "I am sick." You know the words "healthy" and "sick" refer to your body.

You've experienced your body switching from one condition to the other. But what is this "I am"? Why does it stay the same in both cases? What in you stays the same, whether you're healthy or sick? Who in you says "I am"?

You say, "I am clear" or "I am confused." You know the words "clear" and "confused" refer to your thoughts. You've experienced how they change based on your understanding and perspective. But again, there is that "I am" staying the same. Can you recognize the sameness in you, whether you're clear or confused? Can you recognize who says "I am"?

You say, "I am happy" or "I am sad." You know the words "happy" and "sad" refer to your emotions or moods. You've experienced them changing quite often. But there is that "I am" and once again it stays the same no matter what emotion you're feeling. Can you get a sense of the sameness in you, whether you're feeling happy or sad? Can you get a sense of who says "I am"?

You can also extend this practice to all of your experiences. For example, whenever you say "I am this" or "I am that" throughout the day and night, take a moment to ask yourself: who is saying "I am"? Who is having this or that experience? Then you can gradually see for yourself that you are not your experiences. No matter what you're doing or thinking or feeling, you are a being that stays absolutely the same beneath all your experiences.

Another way to practice recognizing this being is to notice your experiences and remind yourself:

"My physical sensations come and go; I don't come and go. I can experience them come and go because I stay the same. My thoughts come and go; I don't come and go. I can experience them come and go because I stay the same. My emotions come and go; I don't come and go. I can experience them come and go because I stay the same." While you notice these different experiences coming and going, you can also notice that you are always present, that you are real, that you *are*.

All these kinds of practices can help you remember that you are a being from God. They can help you carry your true identity with you as you wake in the morning and pray, as you go to work and serve others, as you meet and greet, as you walk and talk, as you eat and drink, as you read and reflect, as you rest and sleep. When you recognize and identify more and more with what you are and less and less with what you're experiencing, you can enter every situation as a blessing and a gift.

Then you can begin to appreciate that this being that you are is your greatest treasure. It is worth more than everything in the heavens and the earth. You don't need to seek this treasure because you already *have* it. You can never lose this treasure because you already *are* it.

After all, how can you ever lose what you are? You are this being long before the first day of your physical life. You are this being when you become a 5-year-old kid. You are this being when you become a 15-year-old teenager. You are this being when you become a 35-year-old adult. You are this being when you become a 65-year-old elder. You are this being on the last day of your physical life and all the days after that one. It stays the same while the rest of you changes over the years. It is the constant among the variables of your life. It is the anchor in the storms of your life. It is the truth of who you really are.

That's why no matter what your circumstances in life might be—whether they are pleasant or unpleasant—they can never disturb or harm or ruin the nature of what God has made you. So whether you are healthy or sick, clear or confused, happy or sad, the being that you are can't be affected by any of it. Since you come from God, there is a holiness about you that can never be touched by the great tragedies and small disappointments of the world. You are always whole, always complete, and always protected.

Give thanks to God who gave you such a gift when he spoke "Be" over you. You not only *have* this gift, you *are* this gift. And no creature, no force, and no circumstance can take it away from you. This is the *being* of "human being" and you refer to it every time you say "I am."

Work on changing your insides by learning that you are a being from God. You are not just a name and a face. You are not what anybody says you are. You are what your maker says you are. You are a spoken word from the mouth of God. So remember who you are by recognizing the being that you are.

Give thanks for it, enjoy it, and let it be the core of your identity.

DECLARE

I am a being from God.
Thank you, God, for speaking "Be" over me.

3

YOU ARE GOOD AND BEAUTIFUL

*He has made everyone and everything
out of beautiful goodness.*

(Quran 32:7)

There is a lie that whispers inside all of us: "There is nothing good in you. There is nothing beautiful about you. You are not important. You have nothing to offer. That is why you are so worthless."

You wish the whispering lie would stop there, but it keeps going: "No one sees you. No one hears you. No one knows you. No one even cares. You are invisible. You are not even real. That is why you are so alone."

At one time or another, we have all believed this lie. We have unintentionally listened to it, accepted it, and let it spread inside us. Even the most confident people have entertained this lie and felt lost in the world. For some, the poison of this lie lasts for hours, maybe even a few days, but then they may recover. For others, it can last for months or even years, making despair a part of their daily lives.

When we believe that no one sees us, we hide ourselves and avoid showing ourselves to other people. When we believe that no one hears us, we get quiet and avoid talking to anyone. When we believe that no one knows us, we reach for distractions and avoid having to know ourselves as well. In this way, we let the lie spread deeper into our minds and hearts.

Sometimes we look to other people to help us overcome the lie. We show up in lots of places so we can be seen. We talk louder so we can be heard. We talk too much in a nervous attempt to make people pay attention to us. But none of this makes any lasting difference. At some point in the evening, the sun goes down, our friends go home, and the fear of being invisible and unimportant rushes right back into us.

Still, we try to convince ourselves that if certain people could see us and hear us and know us in just the right way, we wouldn't feel so invisible. In fact, we could finally feel important. We could finally feel that we are worth paying attention to. To put it another way: "I am nobody until other people think

I am somebody. When other people stop thinking I am somebody, I go back to being nobody." This is what the lie wants us to believe, but God has never made a nobody.

This verse says that God makes everyone out of beautiful goodness. Since God himself is good and beautiful, everyone he makes is good and beautiful—and that includes you. When God said "Be" and spoke you into being, he made you his word. He made you a part of his own language. As a being, you are as good and beautiful as the words of God themselves because you are one of those words. This is how God sees, hears, and knows you. This is how much he treasures you and cares for you. So you are quite real to him and the rest of creation. Give thanks to God for this.

Since you are a word of God, you are somebody. You can't be a nobody. You don't have to ask anybody to make you a somebody. Other people don't get to decide who you are and what you're worth precisely because they didn't make you. Only your maker can decide that, and he has already decided it from the very beginning. You are already somebody by the sheer fact that God decided to make you his word. And what he decided can't be changed or taken away by the shifting opinions of people. Whether people see you, hear you, or know you doesn't make one bit of difference to how good and beautiful you are to God.

So how do you recognize your own beautiful goodness? First, start disagreeing with the lie and speak the truth over it. When it tries to tell you who you are, interrupt it and tell it what God has told you. For example, when the lie tries to tell you that you are not beautiful or that you are worthless, you can talk back and say, "God makes everyone out of beautiful goodness—and that includes me." Speak this truth over every part of your body, every corner of your mind, and every room of your heart. The lie can't hurt the truth, but it can make you forget the truth. That's why everything depends on you remembering the truth of who you are.

Second, start agreeing with God and practice looking for and seeing your own beautiful goodness. Since God has said that you are good, catch yourself being good and doing good. When you are kind, you are doing good. When you are helpful, you are doing good. When you are compassionate, you are doing good. When you are forgiving, you are doing good. Pay attention to how these qualities emerge from inside you when you practice them and you will soon recognize that your goodness is a core part of the being that you are. Then you won't have to believe it because you will know that God put it in you.

Since God has said that you are beautiful, catch yourself being beautiful and doing things that are beautiful. Look in the mirror: you are beautiful. Look at your face, your eyes, your hands, your arms, your legs: they are all beautiful. When you walk or talk, it is beautiful. When you work or play, it is beautiful. When you learn something or make something, it is beautiful. When you stretch your heart, it is beautiful. When you change your mind, it is beautiful. Didn't you know that the beauty that was given to the stars and the trees and the flowers was also given to you? So when you pay attention to where this beauty is coming from, you will soon recognize that it is a core part of the being that you are. Then you won't have to believe it because you will know that God put it in you.

Lastly, spend some time being seen, heard, and known by God. How exactly do you do this? You sit down and you imagine the presence of God all around you. You forget what the lie has been telling you. You forget what other people have been telling you. You let God teach you who you are through your imagination.

When you want to be seen, what you're really wanting is to be seen by God, and he already sees you. He saw you long before he gave you a shape. Sit and imagine him looking at you with great affection and you will begin to get a sense of being seen by him.

When you want to be heard, what you're really wanting is to be heard by God, and he already hears you. He heard you long before he gave you a voice. Sit and speak to God and imagine him listening to you with great interest and you will begin to get a sense of being heard by him.

When you want to be known, what you're really wanting is to be known by God, and he already knows you. He knew you long before you were born. Sit and imagine him embracing you with great compassion and you will begin to get a sense of being known by him.

When you practice imagining that you are seen, heard, and known by God, you begin to see yourself as God sees you: a precious word of his language and a priceless part of his creation. In this way, you can get a sense of your worth and importance directly from God.

Then you can stand in your goodness and beauty, show up in the world, and let yourself be seen. This is not a selfish or arrogant thing to do. This is a blessing and a gift you give to all others. God didn't make you just so you can hide what he made. He made you so you can show his artistry to all of creation.

When birds sing, wolves howl, lightning crackles, and ocean waves roar, they praise God's creativity. They are not showing off. They are showing up in the world to give the gifts God has given them. They are not holding back. They are not embarrassed to make some noise. They are certainly not apologizing for what God has made them—and neither should you.

As much as you need to see, hear, and know your fellow creatures, they need to see, hear, and know you. So show up, speak up, and make yourself known in all the ways that honor the goodness and beauty God has put in you.

Work on changing your insides by learning that God made you out of beautiful goodness. It doesn't matter how long you've been listening to the lie. It doesn't matter how many years you've been waiting for people to make you a somebody. God made you somebody from the moment he made you. He already sees, hears, and knows you as his word. Won't you take the time to see, hear, and know yourself? So recognize your beautiful goodness by practicing your beautiful goodness. It is there and it is strong and it is yours.

DECLARE

I am good and beautiful.
Thank you, God, for making me good and beautiful.

4

YOU ARE FOREVER

*We belong to God
and we are returning to him.*

(Quran 2:156)

When we were little children, we treasured our toys. But a time came when those toys broke or were taken away, and we were miserable.

When we were teenagers, we treasured our clothes and shoes. But a time came when they got ruined or worn out, and we were miserable.

When we became adults, we treasured our careers. But a time came when our careers demanded too many sacrifices or we lost interest, and we were miserable.

Doesn't it make you wonder why this keeps happening? Why do we keep giving our loyalty to things that don't give their loyalty to us? Wouldn't it be amazing if we had something that could never get ruined or worn out? Wouldn't it be wonderful if we had something that could never get lost or taken away from us? We can only ask these kinds of questions because God put in us the desire for a treasure we can always have and keep and enjoy.

We tried to find this treasure among the world's toys, clothes, shoes, jewelry, houses, and careers. But everything in the world has a beginning and an end. Sooner or later, it loses its value and charm. That's why nothing in the world can be the treasure we're looking for. And yet God has hidden it in plain sight. So where exactly is this treasure? It's right where you are.

You yourself are the treasure you have been looking for. God not only gave you such a treasure, he made you such a treasure. The being that you are is the treasure you can always have and keep and enjoy. Since its nature can't be changed, it can never be ruined or worn out. Since it is what you really are, you can never lose it or have it taken away. In fact, God treasures the being that you are so much that he has blessed it with a life that never ends.

This verse says that we belong to God and we are returning to him. When God says "Be" and brings you into being, he is your origin. When God says that you are returning to him, he is your destination. When God says that you belong to him, he is your guardian. This is how he completely surrounds, embraces, and protects your life from all sides. When he gave you the gift of life from his life, he gave you a life that never ends. So the being that you are not only lives, but lives forever and doesn't die. Give thanks to God for this.

A life that never ends is not the usual way we talk about life. We often use phrases like "life and death" where we put life next to death as if they have something in common. We think they are opposites that are related somehow—like up and down, left and right, or night and day. But life is more than the life and death of the body or the mind or the heart.

Life is a quality of God himself. In fact, life (Arabic: al-Hayy) is one of the names of God in the Quran. God is life. He not only lives, but lives forever and doesn't die. Everything that is alive receives a little gift of life from God's life. Such a life is always living. It never stops living. It does not know dying.

That's why life can never be put next to death as if they are opposites. Life is not the opposite of death. Life is one. It has no opposite. The proper opposite of death is birth. What is born, dies. Birth and death go together. Life has nothing to do with either of them. Life puts on a physical form and we call it "birth." Life puts down that physical form and we call it "death." But that life itself lives on forever. Since it was never born, it can never die.

As a being who was given such a life, no harm can ever come to you. Many things can happen to your body, of course. You can break a bone. You can get a disease. You can experience physical death. But since the birth of your body didn't give you life, the death of your body can't take life away from you. When you belong to the God of life, you don't belong to anyone or anything else, especially death. Death doesn't have the power to take your life because death has no power over life. In fact, nothing in the heavens and the earth, nothing in all of creation, can end your life because they have no authority over it. You are never going to die because you are forever.

However, this will not stop certain circumstances in your life from making you think that you are going to die or at least that you are under the threat of death. For example, you can be anxious about your circumstances. You can be afraid of what might happen in the future. You can be filled with regret about the past. You can be disappointed that something you wanted to happen didn't happen. You can feel defeated because you didn't achieve something. You can be full of despair for reasons you don't quite understand.

And yet no matter how painful and overwhelming these circumstances feel to you, they can't kill you. They can't even really defeat you. You may *feel* defeated, but you can't *be* defeated. Why? Because feelings can be raised up by victory and pushed down by defeat, but the being that you are remains untouched and untroubled by victory or defeat. It stays the same no matter what is happening in your world.

Can you think of anything else in your life that has the same qualities? This being can't be lost. It can't be stolen. It can't be ruined. It can't be worn out. It can't fall apart. It can't be cut. It can't be broken. It can't be hurt. It can't bleed. It can't be burned. It can't get weak. It can't get sick. It can't die. That's why the being that you are is a treasure worth more than all the silver and gold and diamonds and pearls in the world. It can never be taken away from you. You can lose everything you have, but you can't lose what you are.

For example, when something happens to your body, like you get hurt or sick, remember who you are. Say, "I am not my body; I have a body. I am experiencing getting hurt. I am experiencing getting sick. But the being that I am is not hurt. The being that I am is not sick. I am whole."

When something happens to your mind, like you get worried or disappointed, remember who you are. Say, "I am not my mind; I have a mind. I am experiencing worry. I am experiencing disappointment. But the being that I am is not worried. The being that I am is not disappointed. I am whole."

When something happens to your heart, like you feel lonely or scared, remember who you are. Say, "I am not my heart; I have a heart. I am experiencing loneliness. I am experiencing fear. But the being that I am is not lonely. The being that I am is not afraid. I am whole."

All this is not to deny that you are going through a difficult experience. That has to be faced and accepted with compassion. What you are trying to do is to make sure that your difficulty doesn't become your whole story. Even in the middle of the pain, there is a part of you that is not in pain. And that part is what can prevent you from getting consumed, overwhelmed, and paralyzed by the pain. By identifying yourself properly with the being that you are, you can pass more easily through your difficulty with courage, wisdom, and grace.

So whenever you find yourself in the middle of difficult circumstances, say, "I belong to God and I am returning to him." Instead of focusing on your troubles, focus on your identity. Remember that the being that you are stays alive forever and never dies. No challenge, no difficulty, and no tragedy can weaken, hurt, or destroy you. You are going to outlast all your troubles. So take a deep breath and smile. Let this give your body, mind, and heart the strength and courage they need to stand up inside your troubles and work to overcome them.

Work on changing your insides by learning that you are forever. This is your share of the good news that life has already overcome death. When God created the sun and the moon and the stars, he put a time limit on them. When God spoke you into being, he put no time limit on you because he created you outside of time. He made you to live forever because he has a long-term investment in you. That's why nothing can end your life. Not earth, water, fire, or air. Not heartbreak or loss. Not embarrassment or rejection. Not depression or delusion. Not fear or death. Your life comes from God's life. And since he is forever, you are forever. Give thanks to God for this.

DECLARE

I am forever.
Thank you, God, for making me live forever.

5

WE ARE ONE

He has made you all out of a single being.

(Quran 7:189)

Suppose a friend of yours invites you to a party. You show up and find yourself in a crowded room. Everyone is already talking to each other. You don't recognize anyone and you don't see your friend yet. What would your first thought be?

A. "I don't know a single person here. I feel uncomfortable. I want to leave."

B. "While I wait for my friend, let me introduce myself to a few people and enjoy the party."

C. "Even if I don't know anyone here, these are all my sisters and brothers. I'm going to meet them as family and see them through God's eyes."

For many of us, our first thought would be to leave (option A). This reflects the basic attitude we've been taught over the years: everyone's a stranger, so be careful and keep your guard up. They might do something to hurt you, so run away and hide. Unless they're already a family member or a friend, the strangeness of other people is our first assumption about them.

When we see strangers, how do we act? We cross our arms and stand in one place, maybe against a wall. We try not to make eye contact and we speak to no one. We're out of our comfort zone. We are literally not ourselves. When we see other people as strangers, we become strangers to ourselves. We forget who we are, so we forget how to talk and smile and express ourselves freely.

Now, instead of wanting to leave, how would we act if we were willing to stay and meet new friends (option B)? We would let our guard down and smile. We would make eye contact, move around the room, and start conversations. We would know that we are safe, so there is no need to run away and hide. In this way, when we see other people as friends, we become friendly ourselves.

Now what if we went even further and saw these people not just as friends, but as sisters and brothers (option C)? You might wonder, how do we do this when they're not actually related to us by blood? Aren't we being overly sentimental and stretching the definition of family a bit too far? Yes, it might be sentimental if it was merely based on fleeting feelings, but it is actually based on the truth. Let me explain.

This verse says that God has made us all out of a single being. This single being is the first creation of God. It is both our mother and father. We are its children. We are all sisters and brothers because we literally have the same parent. All beings are joined together as members of this original family in a real and unsentimental way. And this family of beings is older than the family we're related to by blood.

A long time ago, however, we forgot that we were all family. We became strangers to one another. So today, when we see people, we hide from them. We look away, we push them away, or we run away. We're too guarded to let them enter our lives and too scared to enter theirs.

We like to think that we can build a life with a handful of our favorite people and keep our distance from everyone else. We like to think that we can live isolated from others and still be whole, but no one can be isolated and whole at the same time. In fact, the urge to isolate ourselves is a disease of the mind and heart. It promises to keep us safe, but it actually alienates us from our true family and makes us sick with loneliness and starvation.

This verse offers medicine for that sickness. It is a declaration of the oneness of all humankind. It helps us to start remembering who we really are to each other. It reminds us that we are all one because we are all made out of the same nature. It reminds us that we are all family because we all share the same ancestor. We can't live in isolation because we are made to live together, learn together, and laugh together. We need to see each other. We need to hear each other. We need to know each other. We need to give our gifts to each other and to receive gifts from one another. Only then can our minds and hearts begin to heal from the sickness of isolation. Only then can we see all people as members of the same original family.

So when you walk into a room full of people, make an effort to see them and meet them as your sisters and brothers in being. In the middle of a conversation, for example, you can say to them silently in your mind: "I'm going to look past your name and nationality. I'm going to look past your skin color and clothes. I'm going to look past your opinions and values. I'm going to look past what you've done in the past and what you're doing today. I'm going to see you for who you really are: you are a being from God. You are good. You are beautiful. You are forever. You are my family. I thank God for making you. I am so blessed to meet you."

Would you have trouble doing this for certain people who have a different skin color or come from a different country or believe something different than you? Would you be unwilling to recognize your oneness with them if they didn't look or talk or think just like you? You may have built up walls in your mind and heart to keep people like that out of your life. But you are keeping out members of your own family. These people were made from the same being that you were made from. That means they are just like you. They have been given everything you have been given. They deserve the same level of respect and recognition that you do.

Over the years we have mistakenly learned to use gender, nationality, ethnicity, language, class, and wealth to pretend that we are better than some people and that we have little in common with them. But as long as we refuse to see the truth of who they are, we will not be able to properly see the truth of who we are. Since we all have the same nature, no one is higher or lower than anyone else. No one is more important or less important than anyone else. We are all equal in the eyes of God.

So practice taking down the walls in your mind and heart and welcome your real family with open arms. For example, find a place to sit where different people from all walks of life are walking by, like a park bench or a chair outside a coffee shop. As each person goes by, tell yourself that this person is a fellow being from God and a member of your family. No matter how different they might look to you, look past their faces, clothes, and body language. Look past their bodies, minds, and hearts. Let the being that you are recognize the beings that they are. Let the beautiful goodness in you recognize the beautiful goodness in them.

When an older woman walks by, say to your-self, "This is my aunt." When an older man walks by, say, "This is my uncle." When a woman walks by, say, "This is my sister." When a man walks by, say, "This is my brother." When a young girl and boy walk by, say, "This is my niece and nephew." In this way, you can acknowledge that the members of your ancient family are all around you. You can affirm the unbreakable family bond that you share with every single human being without exception.

The greatest gift you can give to anyone is to help them remember who they are. When you silently remember that the people in front of you are all beings from God and actual members of your own family, somewhere deep inside their minds and hearts, they will begin to remember it too. Even if they can't acknowledge you as a family member, you can still hold and honor the remembrance of who they are in your mind and heart. If you do this every single day with every single person you meet, you will be helping God himself to restore the an-cient memories of your original family, one person at a time.

Work on changing your insides by learning that God made us all out of a single being. Regardless of who your blood family is today, the larger family of all beings is your first family. They were your fam-ily from the very beginning and they will continue to be your family forever. You can never say, "I have no family." Every woman, man, and child is a mem-ber of your family. They are not strangers. They are not only friends. They are your real family, joined with you in being, which is older and stronger than blood.

DECLARE

Everyone is made out of a single being.
Everyone is my family.

6

WE ARE DIFFERENT

O humanity!
Surely, we have created you male and female
and have made you nations and tribes
so you might know one another.

(Quran 49:13)

Suppose you are waiting in a long line to buy some food. There is a person standing in front of you who has a similar height and weight as you, wears similar clothes as you, has the same skin color as you, and comes from the same culture as you. He turns around and mentions something funny about the long line. It makes you laugh. You feel relaxed, knowing that someone like you is sharing your experience of waiting in a long line, so you keep the conversation going.

There is another person standing behind you who has a different height and weight than you, wears different clothes than you, has a different skin color than you, and comes from a different culture than you. She leans forward and mentions something funny about the long line as well. You turn your head just enough to see how different she looks from you. You smile politely and nod your head, but you don't say anything more. You hope she doesn't keep talking to you. While you have to stand in line, you just want to stand in silence and be left alone.

What is it about the similar person that makes us open up? What is it about the different person that makes us shut down? We tend to like those who are like us; we tend to ignore those who are unlike us. Similarity might seem safe and desirable while difference might seem suspicious and undesirable. This is how we tend to see things, but this is certainly not how God sees it.

This verse says that God made us different so we might know one another. It is a declaration of the diversity of all humankind. But how can difference help us know each other when it often drives us apart? There are two ways of understanding difference: either as a wall or a window.

When we see difference as a wall, we are suspicious of people who are different from us. Their difference has nothing valuable to offer us. In fact, we think they are going to take something from us. We don't like seeing their differences, so we avoid them. We are not interested in what we might have in common. We refuse to see them as human beings. We want them to stay in their world and leave us alone to live in our world.

When we see difference as a window, we are curious about the people who are different from us. We think we might learn something from each other. We like seeing variety and diversity, so we appreciate it in the people who are willing to share theirs. We see our common humanity beneath our differences. We want to build a community where many different kinds of people can live, work, and raise their families together.

Where there is a wall, you can't see people, have conversations with them, and get to know them. Where there is a window, you can talk to people, start conversations, and build friendship and community. So difference can only drive us apart if we use it as a wall. But if we use it as a window, it can bring us together in surprising ways and help us learn from one another. Let me explain.

Since we are all beings from God, we share all of the same qualities of being. Due to the physical limitations of the world, however, all these qualities can't be embodied by a single person. They have to be spread out among countless people with a wide range of different thoughts, emotions, skin colors, languages, and cultures. Each one of us embodies a unique combination of these qualities while other people embody other combinations. We are here to teach others about our particular combination and they are here to teach us about theirs. That's why the more people we embrace and welcome into our lives, the more we can all learn about the beings that we are. This is how using difference as a window helps us to know one another.

To better understand how difference enriches our understanding of who we are, let's take the example of light. Light has no color, but when it shows up in the world, it appears as yellow light, red light, blue light, green light, and so on. The colors look different, but they are all different expressions of one light. The light provides the oneness; the colors provide the difference. Oneness and difference in this example work together to help us experience light in all of its colors.

If you could only see shades of red light, you would define light as red. If you added green light next to the red light one day, you would have to change your definition of light so that it includes both red and green. Then you would begin to understand that light itself is colorless, even though it can appear as two different colors. This experience of different colored lights would give you a better understanding of the oneness of light itself. In other words, the experience of difference would give you a better understanding of oneness itself.

Just as recognizing different colors of light helps us understand light itself a little better, recognizing differences among people in the world helps us understand being a little better. God takes the oneness of being and spreads out its qualities across a countless number of different people in the world: women and men; children and elders; brown, black, and white skin; Chinese, Arabic, and French languages; American, African, and Indian cultures; and so on.

In this way, genders, skin colors, languages, and cultures become just a few of the diverse expressions of being. Being is not contained within or defined by any of its expressions, just as light is not defined by any of its colors, but those physical and cultural expressions still offer us windows into being so that we can better appreciate who we are and know one another.

Now let's go back to that person standing behind you in the food line. Knowing what you know now, what could you do differently? You could, for instance, first establish your oneness with her by saying to yourself, "She is a being from God, just like me. She is good and beautiful, just like me. She is important and valuable, just like me. She belongs to the family of beings, just like me. How can I welcome her as a family member and not a stranger? How can I better receive the gift of her oneness with me?"

Then you could appreciate her difference from you by saying to yourself, "If she is an expression of being, like color is an expression of light, how can I better understand those differences? How can I better see her mind and heart? How can I better hear her language and voice? How can I better appreciate her skin color and clothes? How can I better receive the gift of her difference from me?" In this way, a chance encounter with a person who seems different from you can become a deeply meaningful event.

We don't have to ignore, exclude, or be suspicious of someone because they have a different gender, culture, skin color, height, weight, language, perspective, and so on. We don't have to rob ourselves of knowing a person or a group of people that God himself created for us to know. If God sees them and makes them visible, who are we to try to make them invisible and pretend that we don't see them? If God wants them to be here, who are we to want them to be gone? We can't pretend to respect God if we are only interested in respecting the people who look like us while happily ignoring the rest.

Make a commitment to welcoming people who are different from you into your life. Take the time to build close friendships with a variety of people who have different skin colors, who speak different languages, who follow different religions, and who come from different cultures. When you meet someone for the first time, remember that you have been brought together by God to teach each other about the qualities of being that each of you embody. Through this mutual recognition and sharing, you can become windows for each other to better understand the oneness of being and the diversity of its expressions. In this way, you can transform strangers into friends and friends into family.

Work on changing your insides by learning that God made us different so that we might know one another. There are pieces of you that live inside everyone else and there are pieces of everyone else that live inside you. You will never fully understand yourself until you see and hear and know other people through their oneness with you and their difference from you. And they will never fully understand themselves until they see, hear, and know you. If this is how deeply intertwined you are with everyone else, how much do you lose when you turn away from people because they seem different? And yet, how much do you gain when you welcome them and receive the gifts of their oneness and difference?

DECLARE

Difference is a blessing from God.
Difference helps us know one another.

7

WE ARE AMBASSADORS

He has made you all
ambassadors on the earth.

(Quran 6:165)

"Why am I here? What am I supposed to be doing?
Does God want me to become an artist, a teacher,
or a business owner? If only he would give me a sign
and show me the way, then I would know exactly
what I should be doing."

You might find yourself asking these kinds of
questions, especially in moments of failure and
even success. Every failure will make you feel a little smaller and a little less powerful. The sadness it
brings will make you wonder what you're really doing here in the world. Every success will make you

feel a little bigger and a little more powerful. But it will also bring a sadness that will make you wonder if what you're doing matters at all. The sadness of both failure and success might seem unfortunate, but it is actually an invitation to find a more fulfilling sense of meaning, purpose, and direction in your life—if you are willing to listen to it.

Some people think that finding a meaning or purpose in life is some kind of riddle and that we have to come up with an answer that's good enough to unlock it. Until then, we stumble and fumble in the dark, bounce back and forth between failure and success, and try out various things to see if they might fit. And if we are one of the lucky few to figure out that ultimate riddle, then we get the ultimate prize: we get to find meaning, we get to have a purpose, and maybe we even get to feel fulfilled. But what if God didn't make the whole thing to be a riddle so that only a few people can win the prize? What if God has been clear from the very beginning about why we are here and what we're supposed to be doing so that everyone can win the prize?

This verse says that God has made us all ambassadors on the earth. We might wonder, why does God need us to be his ambassadors? To answer this question, let's think about the world of flowers. Even though God can make millions of flowers and spread them across the mountains and valleys and forests of the world, he invites the bees to help him spread the pollen. Can't God spread his own pollen?

Of course, he can. But he assigns this crucial task to one of his humble creatures to fulfill.

In the same way, God invites us to be his ambassadors in the world. He wants us to help him guide humanity, care for the earth, and shape the evolution of his creation by our active participation. When we accept this role and work to fulfill it, we help God unlock the hidden potentials of his own creation, potentials that would have remained hidden if we hadn't been interested in discovering them. The dignity of this appointment and opportunity has been given to every single woman, man, and child on earth—and that includes you. We are all called to represent God's interests and embody his values intentionally and joyfully in the world. And he has made it easy for us to know what these are because he put them right inside us.

When God spoke us into being, he gave us little gifts from his names and qualities. For example, one of the names of God is "the Compassionate" (Arabic: *al-Rahim*). When he introduced us to that name, we received a little gift of compassion from his compassion. This gave us our tremendous capacity for feeling and practicing compassion, mercy, and empathy. Another name of God is "the Knowing" (Arabic: *al-Alim*). When he gave us a little gift from that name, we gained our endless capacity for exploring the unknown, knowing it for ourselves, and making it known to others. In this way, God put all kinds of little gifts from his names and qualities into the very beings that we are.

If we unwrap and explore these little gifts, we become intimately familiar with who God is, what his goals are, and how he wants us to help him. Then we can begin to skillfully represent his interests, embody his values, champion his causes, promote his priorities, and work toward achieving his goals. We do all this not only to guide our personal and family lives, but also to guide the tribes, communities, and societies we live in. Being the ambassadors of God is what gives our lives a meaning, a purpose, and a direction that is not of this world. This is why we're here. This is what we're supposed to be doing.

So how exactly do we do this? Consider, for example, the little gift of compassion that God gave you. You might ask yourself, "How well do I understand what compassion really means? How well do I know how to feel it and practice it and develop it in myself? How do I know when I am resisting compassion and choosing aggression or even apathy? How can I embody compassion more skillfully in my family, among my friends, and within my community? How can I create and support a culture of compassion at work, at school, in government, in business, and in every aspect of society? How can I be an ambassador of compassion on God's behalf?"

As you can tell, this particular quality of compassion is so powerful, it can change not only your life but the character of an entire society. It is up to the ambassadors of God, like you, to do the work to embody it in yourself and champion it in the world. Then it can show up inside individuals and societies as a living fact and not just as a future aspiration. In the same way, you can orient everything you think, say, and do around the various names and qualities of God because he put little gift-sized versions of all of them inside you.

That's why it doesn't really matter if you're an artist, a teacher, or a business owner. One is not more dignified than the other. What matters is the degree to which you fulfill your role as ambassador while you do whatever you do. You can be an ambassador of God working as an artist if you inspire your sisters and brothers to become creative in their own lives. You can be an ambassador of God working as a teacher if you help your students to not just learn their lessons, but to use what they learn to serve others. You can be an ambassador of God working as a business owner if you see your employees as beautiful beings from God who bring many unique gifts to their work. In this way, you can carry your role as ambassador into every occupation, every situation, and every relationship—at all times and in all places.

Keep in mind that not everyone will fulfill their role as an ambassador of God. Some people will abuse it and become tyrants. Others will refuse it and become tourists. A tyrant is someone who thinks he owns the earth, so he seizes the land and dominates the people. God wants him to be an ambassador, but he wants to be a ruler. A tourist is someone who knows he doesn't own the earth, so he merely passes through the land and tries not to disturb the people. God wants him to be engaged, but he's afraid to get involved.

Beyond the aggressive position of the tyrant and the passive position of the tourist, you can take a compassionately engaged position as an ambassador of God. You are not here to be the center of the world and impose your will on others, like a tyrant. You are also not here to sit on the sidelines, keep quiet, and pass unnoticed in the world without upsetting anyone, like a tourist.

You can see yourself as a gardener of the earth. You take responsibility for the garden. You know you don't own it. You care for it on behalf of someone who does own it. You know that you can't do whatever you want with it. You use the little gifts of God's names and qualities inside you to work, to contribute, to make a difference. You serve the owner's best interests and the garden's highest potential with humility and enthusiasm. And that's how you fulfill the role God has given you.

Work on changing your insides by learning that God made you an ambassador on earth. Your purpose and your work in the world aren't buried inside riddles. And you won't find meaning in merely achieving success and avoiding failure. The way to fulfillment is to fulfill the role God has given you—intentionally, skillfully, joyfully. So be an ambassador of God with your whole mind and heart. Claim this role, take ownership of it, and commit to it. Adopt the values of God as your own so you can embody them personally and champion them socially. Let this bring you meaning, purpose, and fulfillment of a kind that mere success knows nothing about. This is not something you have to do; this is something you get to do. Give thanks to God for this.

DECLARE

I am an ambassador of God.
I represent his interests on earth.

8

GOD IS ONE

There is no god but God.

(Quran 47:19)

We didn't create ourselves: that is a fact. We didn't throw the mountains and oceans together and make the world. We didn't fill the forests with falcons and wolves and bears. We didn't put art and music and storytelling inside people so they might delight in them. All this was already here before we got here. We didn't make any of it. So who did?

In ancient times, we believed the gods made the world. What is a god? Any individual or force that we believe is more powerful than us and that can influence the events in our lives so we are motivated to bring all our hopes and fears to it.

For example, the stories of the Indian, Greek, and Norse gods and goddesses mention how one god controlled the weather and another goddess commanded the sea. One goddess cared for the animals and another god invented writing and poetry. One goddess might bring good fortune. Another god might be cruel and bring misery. One was in charge of life, another in charge of death.

Through stories and symbols, we gave these gods personalities and histories. Through rituals and sacrifices, we tried to win their protection and favors. We laid all our hopes and fears at their feet. When our hopes came true, we thought we had earned their pleasure. When our fears came true, we thought we had angered them.

Since each god was in charge of a different part of creation, each cared only about their specific part. So they argued and fought with each other, just like us. They competed for power and influence, just like us. And they were never satisfied and always wanted more, just like us. Creation was the result of the conflicts among the gods. The world was divided because the gods who made it were divided.

Since we were made by these gods, we found ourselves to be divided as well. Our fears fought with our hopes and our hopes were afraid of our fears. The forces within our minds and hearts pulled and pushed in different directions. We took our hopes and fears to many different gods. We said one thing, but did another. We thought one thing, but felt another. We wanted one thing, but knew we should

want another. In this way, we were deeply frag-
mented, easily distracted, and ultimately destruc-
tive. The gods were at war. The world was at war.
We were at war. So divided were we, how could we
ever be whole?

Then a new line of teachers began to appear. We
called them our prophets and sages. They taught us
that all division is actually an illusion. The world
appears to be divided, but beneath all the conflicts,
there is a unity. Instead of many gods, there is only
one God. They introduced us to the principle of
oneness: one creator creating one creation. This
principle seemed too good to be true and too simple
to accept. And yet it marked the beginning of the
end of all division everywhere.

This verse says that there is no god but God
(Arabic: *la ilaha illallah*). This is possibly the most
concise declaration of the oneness of God. There
is one and only one God. There are no other gods.
He has no peers or partners. He has no ancestors or
children. He alone put the heavens and the earth
together. He alone is in charge of all creatures, all
forces, and all things.

Since God spoke us all into being, he alone is the
Being of all beings. He *is* the source and foundation
of who we *are*. There is no strength, no help, and no
mercy other than his. Whether we acknowledge it
or not, all beings depend on him for life, identity,
purpose, nourishment, protection, attention, and
affection.

The principle of his oneness stretches into all of creation. Since God is one, the world he makes is one and the people he puts in it are also one. Even though the mountains and the oceans and the stars look different, they still share an underlying unity. Even though people come from different backgrounds and act in different ways, they still share the same nature.

Despite all of this, we are still conflicted. We are still at war inside ourselves. Our minds and hearts still look to multiple things, different people, and specific circumstances to satisfy our hopes and protect us from our fears. For example, there are things we hope for and things we wish would come true. There are other things we fear and things that would trouble us greatly if they came to pass. Or there are certain people we take our hopes and fears to so that they might help us fulfill our hopes and avoid our fears.

In other words, we throw ourselves at the mercy of things, people, and circumstances. We look to them to deliver us from our troubles. We treat them like little gods. So even though we might agree with the concept of one God, we might still be appealing to a number of false gods to help us out of our problems. This takes us out of alignment with the oneness of God and his creation. This divides our minds and scatters our hearts. This is what creates the conflict and war inside us.

So how do you unite your mind and heart and commit yourself to the oneness? You remember and affirm God's oneness: "There is no god but God." This reminds you that God gave you a little gift from his oneness (Arabic: *al-Ahad*). The being that you are is one; it is not made of separate parts. Even though you may *feel* conflicted, you can never *be* conflicted. Different parts of your mind and heart may pull you in different directions and create immense confusion and conflict. But the being that you are is always whole, free of conflict, and aligned with the oneness everywhere.

So if we are whole as beings but still conflicted in our minds and hearts, there is a gap between what we really are and how we actually feel. How do we close that gap? By training our minds and hearts to understand, feel, and practice the principle of oneness. As hopes and fears come up in your life, take them immediately to God. Start talking to God about them. Tell him what you secretly desire. Show him what you privately fear. Then he will guide you to take the next step, to do the practical thing, or to talk to the right person.

This is not about praying for everything and doing nothing. This is about making sure the first movement of your mind and heart is a movement toward God. It's about trusting and depending on God as the first and foremost source for all your solutions. And then you can take the practical steps he inspires you to take.

By focusing only on the one God, the mind can overcome its divided attention. By devoting itself only to the one God, the heart can overcome its scattered affection. This doesn't mean that the variety of forces inside us stop fighting and melt into one. They maintain their valuable differences, but now they are like players in a symphony following the lead of a single conductor. Since they look to God for everything, it unifies and harmonizes them and closes the gap.

In these small daily steps of leaning toward God and referring everything to God, you can remind yourself that there is no god but God. It is God who creates everything in the heavens and the earth for you. It is God who powers the workings of your mind and heart and body. It is God who teaches and heals you. It is God who solves your problems and clears your way. And it is God who deserves your thanks and praise.

As you start thinking in this way, you find that your awareness of God's presence and activity in your life becomes stronger and stronger. You live surrounded by the strength and care of God in everything you say and do. This gives your life a certain kind of unity and harmony. You no longer take your major and minor hopes and fears to a thousand different little things in your world. You keep bringing them back over and over to the God who causes all things to be what they are and to work as they do.

Work on changing your insides by learning that there is no god but God. Every single day you have to choose who receives all your hopes and fears. And that choice reaffirms who it is that you really worship and follow. So choose God. When you focus on him, he gathers up the divided attention of your mind and the scattered affection of your heart and unites them. Like a magnet that suddenly seizes and draws scattered bits of iron to itself, God magnetically draws your mind and heart to himself. All your old loyalties, conflicts, and divisions gradually lose their hold on you. As you become more single-minded and whole-hearted in your devotion to God, you discover your own oneness through the remembrance of his oneness. This is the beginning of the end of the war inside yourself.

DECLARE

There is no god but God.
I bring all my hopes and fears to him.

9

GOD IS A TEACHER

Recite!
in the name of your Lord who created,
created you all from a clot.
Recite!
and your Lord is the most Generous,
who taught by the pen,
taught you all what you did not know.

(Quran 96:1-5)

Do you remember the first time you learned about God? What stories were you told about him? What role did he play in those stories? Was he distant or near, judgmental or compassionate, mysterious or familiar? What kind of image did that create in your mind about God?

For many people, God is described as a judge who judges us harshly from a distance. He gives us trials and temptations and waits for us to fall down. He seems to be looking for a reason to criticize and condemn us. Nothing we do is ever good enough for him.

Some religious leaders use this harsh image of God to threaten their followers to stay inside their religious traditions out of fear. Of course, as people mature in their understanding, threats of punishment don't work anymore. They leave their religious traditions and even religion altogether over this distorted image of God. They don't often return because many traditions don't offer any alternatives.

This verse says that our creator is also our teacher. It paints in our minds the image of an incredible creator who creates our complex physical bodies out of the smallest pieces of flesh: a cell, a zygote, an embryo. This verse extends the image of a creator into the image of a teacher who teaches our complex minds and hearts what they did not know.

What all this tells us is that God is an artist, an architect, a craftsman, and a scientist. He shows himself to us through his revelations and creations. What this also tells us is that God is a giver of knowledge, a teacher of reading and writing, a builder of schools, and a patron of learning. God shares his thoughts and ideas with us through his lessons and teachings.

Of all the things that God could have said as his first words to the Prophet Muhammad, he chose to say that he is our creator and teacher. He created us to teach us, not to judge us and reject us. This is a real alternative to the distorted image of God as a harsh judge of our mistakes. So if God is more like a teacher and less like a judge, doesn't that change everything? Doesn't that make God more approachable than ever before? Doesn't that cast what we're doing here on earth in a much kinder light? Let's take a look at the creation story as an example of what this could mean.

Once upon a time, God created the first woman and the first man. They both lived in a garden where they were given everything they needed. God told them to enjoy the garden, but he forbid them to eat from one particular tree. So they avoided that tree until they started talking to a stranger in the garden. He claimed to have knowledge that God did not share with them and offered to teach them. He told them to eat from the tree because it would give them more knowledge than they ever had before. So they ate from the tree and it changed their minds and hearts. God noticed the change and told them to go down to the earth for a time. Instead of being given everything they needed, they would have to work for everything they wanted there.

Some people take this story as evidence of our brokenness and disobedience. They claim that by eating from the forbidden tree, we sinned against God. And he was so angry that he threw us down to the earth, turned his face away, and refused to talk to us. This is how he punished us for our original sin of disobeying him. Today we are all here, doing time on earth, roughing it with the birds and the beasts in search of food and water, trying to survive and hoping God will take us back after we die.

However, if God is a teacher and we are his students, then there are other ways of interpreting this story. For example, when God forbid the first woman and first man to eat from this one particular tree, it was less of a warning and more of an assessment. God wanted to evaluate their ability to understand, to keep their agreements, to follow directions, and to listen to the right teacher. When they listened to a false teacher and followed his advice, they became his students and forgot that they were students of God. They switched teachers without fully understanding the consequences of what they were doing. They didn't have a clear way to distinguish between a true teaching and a false teaching. They didn't commit a sin; they made a learning mistake. After all, the garden was their learning environment.

As a consequence of this mistake, God didn't necessarily punish them. He relocated them to a different learning environment that was more appropriate for their level of understanding. Isn't that what a teacher does? If a student is not able to grasp the lessons at a particular grade level, the teacher can move him to a different grade level where he can take his time to learn. This is not punishment, but compassionate education. Does it make any sense that God would create students who initially know very little and then punish them severely for not knowing more than the little they know? So even though they weren't able to follow his advice in the garden, God wants them to learn how to follow it on earth.

What this means is that we are not broken. As beings, we are always whole. And in our minds and hearts, we are students who are always learning, making mistakes, and learning from our mistakes—all inside the vast classrooms of our creator and our teacher. What this also means is that both the garden and the earth are two different kinds of lush learning environments. The earth is not a prison. It is not a punishment for getting it wrong in the garden. The earth is a different kind of garden, where our role as students and God's role as teacher continues.

How do we know this? The Quran says over and over again that God created all the things on earth for us. He appointed the day for our work and the night for our rest. He hung the sun and the moon to light our way. He raised the sky as a canopy and spread out the hills. He populated the world with all kinds of life. He showed us the path of right and wrong. The Quran mentions all these things and then it says that these are all signs of God for those who think and reflect on them. Does a jailor create this type of lush environment for his prisoners? God has not sent us to the earth to punish us and to make us feel bad for a learning mistake our ancestors made. He sent us to the earth to continue our education as an act of kindness and compassion.

So how do you choose God as your first teacher before every other teacher? If you are reading something, for example, and you don't understand what it says, ask God first to explain it to you as you re-read it. If you are trying to solve a math problem and you get stuck, ask God to show you the next step before you search through the examples in your math book. If you are having an argument with someone, ask God to teach you how to listen closely to the other person, speak thoughtfully with them, and reconcile. If you are having trouble accepting why some difficulty is happening in your life, ask God to share his wider perspective of the situation with you.

If you let God teach you throughout the day and night like this, you will find the lines of communication opening up between you and him. If you put your attention on him and receive his attention on you, God will inspire answers inside you or lead you to the answers. So talk to God like you would talk to your teacher. Let your mind be a student of God's mind. God wants to teach you what you don't know. He wants to make the unknown known to you. He wants you to know him through his creation and his creativity. In this way, you can build a close relationship with God in which he truly is your teacher and you truly are his student and the earth is truly a lush learning environment.

Work on changing your insides by learning that God is a kind teacher, not a harsh judge. He is holding every cell in your body together so you can have all the learning experiences that you are having in this world. This is a sign of kindness, not harshness. So choose him as your first and most important teacher. Ask him to teach you and guide you not only in the major events in your life, but also in the small matters as well. Come to him with a curious mind and an eager heart. Let him teach you every single thing you have ever wanted to learn.

DECLARE

God is my teacher.
I am his student.

10

GOD IS A FRIEND

God is the friend of those who believe.

(Quran 2:257)

Do you have an old friend you haven't talked to in a long time? Maybe you went to school with this friend or you worked together for years. But then you stopped doing things together or you moved away. You lost touch and drifted apart. Years later, you think about your friend sometimes and wonder how they're doing. You wish you could get back in touch and it would be like old times. But maybe too much time and distance has passed. You're both living such different lives. Maybe the opportunity for reconnecting with your friend is over.

A long time ago, God was our friend. He was our first friend. He made us and held us and cared for us. In those early days, we could hear him and talk to him. We really enjoyed being so close to him. Sometime later, our minds got fascinated with other things and forgot him. Our hearts felt drawn to other things and turned away from him. Year after year, we learned to live without his closeness and his conversations.

We learned to live alone in the house of our own mind and heart. The rooms were decorated with beautiful furniture and fixtures. As we walked through them, they made us sad, but we didn't know why. Sometimes we heard a noise and thought we might come across another person, but it was only the wind moving over the waters outside. We learned to accept that there is no one in the house except us. No one told us that we were living alone like this because we might have uninvited God from our lives.

This verse says that God is the friend of those who believe. God has always been more than our creator and teacher. He has been our friend from the moment he made us. Even when we stopped being his friend, he kept being our loyal friend. He doesn't want to keep his distance from us as a typical lord might keep with his servant. He is closer to us than anyone else, so he wants us to be closer to him than everyone we know.

This intimate friendship with God feeds and nourishes every part of our lives, providing sanity to our minds and satisfaction to our hearts. That's why God is always inviting us to return to that friendship. He asks that we take down the walls in our minds and hearts that have been keeping him out. He asks that we invite him back in. It doesn't matter that we drifted away from him. It doesn't matter how many years have passed. The opportunity for reconnecting is never over. This friendship can be renewed any time.

You might be wondering: given how different God is from the rest of us, is there any real possibility of actually contacting him, much less communicating with him? How can you talk to someone who doesn't have eyes or a face or a body? How can you relate to someone who doesn't have any of the hopes and fears that you do? How do you spend time with someone who is beyond time? How can you be friends with someone you can't see or hear or touch? These are all good questions.

The first thing to remember is that God said "Be" and made us beings out of his own speech. We come directly from him. This gives us a permanent and unbreakable relationship with him from the very beginning. This also allows us to connect and communicate with him now and forever. The second thing is that he put his names and qualities inside us. This allows us to recognize, understand, and appreciate him to the degree that we embody those names and qualities. The third thing is that God desires to be friends with us. That means he created us with the capacity and desire to be friends with him.

So the possibility of actually being friends with our creator is quite real and natural.

Think about a good friend you have right now. What you cherish about that person is not necessarily their eyes or face or body. What you cherish is their mind, their heart, the very being that they are. You appreciate and value the attention and affection you exchange with each other. Your friendship with them is happening between your joined minds and hearts. It is happening between the being that you are and the being that they are. In other words, your entire relationship with them is based on all the things about them that are beyond their physical or material form. And the same goes for your friendship with God.

This may go against some of our cultural conditioning, but it doesn't go against the truth of who we are. "God might be a nice idea to believe in," some might say, "but God is so distant and beyond us that it's not practical to actually be friends with him. It sounds extreme, even a little silly." But this is exactly why some people feel so cold and distant about God. They have abstracted him right out of their lives. "He might be out there somewhere," they speculate, "but he's certainly not interested in what's going on in my life."

The prophets and sages, however, beg to differ. Adam, Noah, Abraham, David, Solomon, Moses, Mary, Jesus, and Muhammad are close friends of God. In fact, the Quran explicitly calls Abraham a "friend of God" (Arabic: khalil allah). God is intimately involved and interested in their lives. They couldn't have done all the things they did if they hadn't renewed their friendship with God. So they encourage us to renew that same friendship because we were all made to be friends with God, just like them.

So how do you start? You start your friendship with God in the same way you start any friendship: you invite him over, you talk to him, and you spend time in each other's company. He is the presence that surrounds the house of your mind and heart, but does not enter uninvited. So slide the curtains apart, push the windows out, and swing the front door wide open. Feel the wind caress your face and blow through your house. Welcome your friend back into your life. And don't just let him sit in the living room like a guest. Tell him the best room in the house is his if he wants it. Tell him that you would be honored if he would stay as long as he likes. When you invite God back into your mind and heart in this way, you are inviting him to take up permanent residence in your life.

Once you've invited him in, talk to God like he is your best friend. Thank him for his blessings and favors. Share your hopes and fears with him. Ask him for advice and guidance. Then listen to him. Visualize your mind like an empty cup that he can fill with new ideas, new perspectives, and new inspirations. Just listen, stay open, and wait. Sometimes you will receive something, other times you won't, but that's not important. What's important is that you keep the lines of communication open and practice your friendship with him through these kinds of intimate conversations.

God is the kind of friend who can be with you every hour of every day and night. He never needs to leave you and go home. He's never got something better to do. He is always and forever with you. He is always talking to you, caring for you, teaching you how to care for his creation, and accompanying you in every experience. Since God is always with you, learn to always be with God. No matter what you're doing, imagine that he is with you, within you, and all around you. Invite him to join you in everything you do.

Keep him first and foremost in your mind and heart. When you have successes in your life, tell him about it first and thank him for his blessings and support. When you have struggles or misfortunes in your life, tell him about it first and ask for his strength and courage and patience. When you identify a goal you want to reach, tell him about it first and ask for his help and guidance. Ask him also about his own goals and how you can help him. When you make mistakes or you have hurt someone, tell him about it first and ask him for his forgiveness as well as how you can apologize and reconcile with the person you hurt. In this way, share everything with him and hide nothing from him. Let your heart be a friend of God's heart.

Work on changing your insides by learning that God is a friend, not a stranger. Your constant companionship with your creator is normal, natural, and necessary. When the mind and heart forget about God's friendship and try to live alone in the world without him, that is not normal or healthy. So invite him back into the house of your mind and heart. Include your best friend in everything you do. As you direct your affections toward him, you receive more fully his affections toward you. In this way, you can let God draw you nearer and nearer to him in a mutual friendship that grows and lasts forever.

DECLARE

God is my friend.
I am his friend.

THEN, PRACTICE

11

REMEMBER GOD

Surely in the remembrance of God
do hearts find peace.

(Quran 13:28)

If you take a fish out of the river and put it on dry land, what will it do? It will start to flop around desperately. It will throw its little body up in the air, twisting and turning, hoping to fall back into the river it was just swimming in.

Now suppose someone says to you, "Let's put that fish in olive oil. He'll be fine." What do you think will happen? You know that fish will die. Or suppose someone says, "Let's put that fish in orange juice. He'll be fine." What do you think will happen? Again, that fish is going to die.

You can't put a fish in something that is foreign to it and expect it to survive. It simply can't live and breathe in olive oil or orange juice. Since the fish comes from river water, it needs that kind of water to survive and thrive; even ocean water won't help. If it doesn't get back to its original water, it will die.

This verse says that in the remembrance of God, our minds and hearts find peace. Just like the fish needs to be immersed in river water to live, your mind and heart need to be immersed in the remembrance of God's presence to thrive. Only then can you find the peace that comes from God.

God is everywhere. He is inside you and he is outside of you. Better yet, you are inside him. You are always surrounded and immersed in his presence. You can never live outside of his presence. No matter where you go, God is there. No matter what you are doing, God is with you. In fact, God *is* where you *are.*

God's presence sends out his blessings and gifts, his graces and mercies, to all of his creatures and creations—at all times and in all directions. As a being, you are grounded in God's presence because you come from him and you belong to him. That means God's blessings—in the form of life, will, intelligence, wisdom, creativity, strength, nourishment, courage, compassion, joy, well-being, and countless others—are always available to you. As a being, you have full access to the peace of God at all times and under all circumstances.

Your mind and heart, however, work a little differently. They are limited to having only partial access to the blessings of God. And they can only have this partial access if they keep their focus on God. In other words, they must work for it. The mind and heart have to make a deliberate effort to become aware of his presence and to stay aware of it as much as they can. If they completely forget God, by getting distracted by other things or outright choosing to ignore him, then the mind and heart block most of his peace and nourishment from reaching you. A small trickle may still make its way through, but it's barely enough.

So the being that you are receives God's blessings effortlessly while the mind and heart that you have must make an effort to receive them. This might explain how you can feel blessed and grateful at your core and yet still worried and anxious in your mind and heart—all at the same time. This division inside yourself can be quite painful, but there is a remedy for it.

The practice of the remembrance of God (Arabic: dhikr) conditions our minds and hearts to begin to feel the presence of God once again. It opens us to receive the food and water we need from God. It allows us to receive more and more of God's blessings and gifts. It inspires us to move in the world with strength and courage and purpose. It aligns the beings that we are with the minds and hearts that we have so that we can feel undivided and whole in ourselves.

So what is the remembrance of God all about? It's not about remembering something that happened in the past. It's not about remembering that God created the universe and sent the prophets. It's not about remembering that God looks down on us from somewhere up there beyond the clouds.

Remembrance is actually about imagining that God is with us, right here and right now. It's about feeling that we are surrounded and immersed in his presence. It's about becoming aware of the actual presence of God in the room we are sitting in, on the road we are walking on, in the body we are wearing, in the minds and hearts we are inhabiting. It's about recognizing his active involvement in our lives as he feeds us, teaches us, and cares for us. It's about actually trying to make contact with the creator, to open up the lines of communication, so that we can have a continuous conversation with him.

So how exactly do you practice the remembrance of God? There are many ways, of course, but there are two main ways for an individual to practice. The first way is where you remember God alone and forget everything else. This is where you stop everything you are doing and sit for at least five minutes and focus only on him. You give him your undivided attention, without any other distraction. You temporarily put aside all other cares and concerns and immediately find his peace. This is your one-on-one time with God. The world can wait.

The second way of practicing is where you remember God in the background of your mind and heart while you perform your daily activities in his presence. This is where you make an effort to remember God all the time, in every waking hour of the day and night, no matter what you're doing. You imagine that he is with you as you wake up in the morning, brush your teeth, put on your clothes, go to work or school, talk with a friend, eat lunch, attend a meeting, make dinner, wash dishes, read a book, and fall asleep for the night. By bringing God with you into your world, you maintain that constant contact with him and find his peace.

In both of these practices, you can recite one of the names of God intentionally to help you focus your mind and heart on him. In the Quran, for example, God has 99 names. Each one of them describes one of his qualities. You might pick one of these names, like "the Caring" (Arabic: *al-Rahman*), and recite it like this: "ya Rahman, ya Rahman..." which means something close to "you are so Caring, you are so Caring...." You can recite this out loud or softly or silently in your mind and let it keep pulling your attention back to God. You're not trying to recite this mechanically or mindlessly. You're trying to recite the name deliberately and reflect on its meaning.

For instance, you can think about all the ways God has cared for you over the years. You can take this opportunity to offer your heartfelt thanks to him for his caring. You can also ask him to bless specific people that come to mind with his caring. You can also ask that he show you where you could be more caring toward others in your own life. In this way, you can use the recitation of the name to create an atmosphere of being in God's presence and having conversations with him.

As you go deeper into this practice of remembrance, there will be times when you don't feel like saying anything. You just want to sit with your creator, your teacher, your friend. You just want to bask in the presence of God. And you can do just that. You can just enjoy his company. You can imagine his hand resting over your hand.

You can be vulnerable with him. You can trust him. He has more affection for you than any creature in the heavens and the earth. So let him in. Let him enter your mind and heart and show him all the hidden corners. Show him who you really are and let him smile upon you. Feel his smile upon every part of your body, every corner of your mind, and every room of your heart. Smile back.

Work on changing your insides by learning that in the remembrance of God you find peace. When you remember God, he helps you remember who you are. He gives you the proper food and water you need to keep your mind and heart healthy and strong. When you forget God, you also forget yourself. Your heart sinks into sadness and your mind falls into desperation. The being that you are doesn't change, of course, but your mind and heart do lose their access to all the blessings and gifts God has stored in it. Yet it can all be restored to you as soon as you immerse your mind and heart in the remembrance of God once again. Just as the fish can't make a life for itself outside of water, you can't survive and thrive outside of a real awareness of God's presence. So remember God always and receive the daily bread of his peace.

DECLARE

I remember God day and night.
I find his peace day and night.

12

GIVE THANKS TO GOD

Give thanks to God.
Those who give thanks,
give thanks
for their own benefit.

(Quran 31:12)

Why is it so hard to give thanks to God? Of course, it's easy to say "thank you" to each other as a part of everyday conversation because other people are saying it to us. But why is it so hard to give thanks to God with a genuine feeling of gratitude and appreciation behind it? Why does it bring up all kinds of resistances?

Some of us find it hard to give thanks to God because we might be resentful about a number of things we didn't get in life. Certain people or certain things or certain experiences never came into our lives the way they came into the lives of others. And that resentment blocks us from appreciating all the blessings that God did bring into our lives. Why should we be thankful, we wonder, for a life that feels so incomplete?

Others of us find it hard to give thanks to God even though we got most of the things we wanted in life. We got to enjoy many privileges and advantages that others never had. Even when we were taught to give thanks to God, a tiny whisper told us, "You worked pretty hard to get where you are. You earned it. You deserve it. No one ever gave you anything." Why should we give thanks for any of it now, we wonder, especially when it seems so unnecessary to our success?

This verse calls us to give thanks to God and reminds us that it is only for our own benefit. God doesn't need our thanks because he is free of all needs. We, however, need to be thankful because we are in need of him. Being thankful is the fundamental way a creature can respond to the creator for having been created. It helps us recognize God as the lead actor and director of our lives and ourselves as the supporting cast.

We can't do anything by ourselves. We can't get anything we need by ourselves. We need God for everything. If we can acknowledge our dependence on him, then we can see and hear and feel how much he is involved in our lives in the most caring and compassionate way. This recognition can bring into our minds and hearts an experience of genuine gratitude and heartfelt appreciation toward him.

But if we resist this recognition and deny our dependence on him, then we fall into the trap of thinking that we alone are the author and agent of our success. In fact, we might even refuse to acknowledge that we are created and supported by him at all. Then we can pretend that he is absent from our lives and we can play the role of God ourselves.

For example, when we believe that our lives are hopeless because we didn't get many of the things we wanted and there's nothing anyone can do about it, we are playing God. When we think that all of our accomplishments are the result of our own efforts, we are playing God. When we make all of our decisions by ourselves without asking God for his guidance, we are playing God. In these ways, we are refusing to be properly thankful because we don't want to stop playing God.

This, of course, creates a great deal of pain, suffering, and delusion. It narrows our minds and shrinks our hearts so that we can't properly receive the blessings and gifts of God. We pretend that we can live like this for a long time, but no one can live and thrive with a lie as large as this one.

At a certain point, however, we might realize that what we really want is not to play God, but to belong to God. We want to be a part of something much larger than ourselves. And that's when the truth becomes much sweeter and more attractive than any lie. That's when we stop resisting God and start thanking him. To give thanks is to admit that we are not God. To give thanks is to admit that God is the creator and we are the creatures, just as it should be.

So how exactly do you give thanks to God? You can only give thanks for the things you can appreciate. You have to be able to see it, feel it, understand it, or imagine it to give thanks for it. If you don't know about it, you can't be thankful for it. So the first step is to start noticing what's going on in your life and start appreciating it.

Start small. Start with your body. You may not be in great health, but what parts of your body are working just fine? Look at your hands, for example. Lift your hands up in front of your eyes and take a whole minute to slowly look at them. Can you imagine how many atoms and molecules, skin and bones, nerve and blood cells God has to orchestrate to work just right for you to open and close your hands? There are people whose hands don't work. There are people who don't have hands. But your hands work just fine. Give thanks to God for this. Repeat this exercise with other parts of your body.

Now think about your family. You may not have a great relationship with all the members of your family, but are there some individuals in your family that have given you a great deal of affection and support? Imagine them standing in front of your right now, whether they are physically alive today or they have passed on. Can you tell them what they did for you and what it meant to you? Can you

thank them for their involvement in your life? Give
thanks to God for them and ask God to bless them.
Repeat this exercise with other people that come to
mind.

Now think about your home. You may not have
the fanciest place to live, but are there some things
about it that you can appreciate? Look around at all
the things you have. Look through all the rooms.
Look at your clothes and shoes. Look at where you
eat, sleep, and relax. Where do you enjoy being the
most in your home? Can you remember some fond
memories in your home? Did you ever have to leave
your home for a time and found yourself missing
it? Give thanks to God for all this. Repeat this exercise with anything else that comes to mind about
your home.

Now think about the being that you are. Have
you ever just sat down and thought about the fact
that God made you? Let's slow it down and repeat it:
God...made...you. The God who made the sun, the
moon, and the stars made you. The God who made
the forests, the mountains, and the oceans made
you. The God who made Moses, Mary, Jesus, and
Muhammad made you. The God who made countless upon countless beings still made one more:
you. Despite a very busy schedule caring for every
creature across the heavens and the earth and beyond, God still took the time to make you. Take this
as personally as you possibly can. And give thanks
to God for making you.

Then you can begin to realize that just being created by God is the best thing that could ever have happened to you. From the moment God brought you into being, you won the lottery. You got God. You got being. You got a huge family of beings. You got blessings. You got gifts. You got a vast and beautiful creation to explore. And you are not going to lose any of these things because you got them to enjoy forever. For just one moment, for just one single second, let yourself feel this fact and get giddy about it. And then give thanks to God like you mean it.

Look for God's gifts in every thing you see, in every person you meet, in every experience you have—and give thanks for all of it. When you start paying attention to what God has already given you, you begin to understand that you are already rich with blessings and gifts from day one. Of course, you may still want certain people or things or experiences to come into your life, but you can also acknowledge that God has already given you the best of all that is worth having. Your cup is quite full. Appreciate that first and then seek to add to it wisely.

Work on changing your insides by learning that giving thanks to God brings you tremendous benefits. You are not just giving thanks because it's a nice thing to say. You give thanks to affirm and reinforce your relationship with God. You give thanks out of simple respect, courtesy, and affection for him. And you don't just give thanks to him once or twice, here or there, or on special occasions. You give thanks to him all the time, day and night. By putting yourself into a state of appreciation, curiosity, and delight, you learn to see everything throughout the day and night through the eyes of gratitude. In this way, giving thanks to God becomes not just an occasional practice, but a way of life.

DECLARE

Thank you, God.
Thank you for every single blessing
you bring into my life.

13

STUDY GOD'S SIGNS

Surely, in the creation
of the heavens and the earth,
and the difference of night and day,
and the ships running upon the sea,
and the rain God sends down from the sky,
reviving the earth after its death,
and the spreading of all kinds of creatures,
and the winds and the clouds
between heaven and earth:
these are all signs of God
for a people who think.

(Quran 2:164)

If you want to appreciate the architecture of one of the greatest architects, Zaha Hadid (1950-2016), you can't just stare at a few striking photographs of her buildings. You have to research her projects, her design process, and her impact on her field at large.

If you want to understand the philosophy of one of the greatest philosophers, Ibn Arabi (1165-1240), you can't just read a few precious quotes from him. You have to undertake a close study of his main philosophical and poetic writings and their impact on later generations.

If you want to understand the creator of the heavens and the earth a little better, you can't just read the Quran or the Gospels or the Torah. You have to investigate as far as you can the surfaces and depths of all the worlds, creatures, and cultures God has made. In other words, if you want to understand the artist, you have to study his artwork in great and thorough detail.

This verse says that God created everything in the heavens and the earth and filled it with his signs for a people who think. God is not some distant figure who stands apart from the world. He is always present and intimately involved with the world. In fact, God wants to be known. That's why he has poured his names and qualities into every aspect of the world. The world is a book that contains the signs of God. If we study this book closely, we can learn to read those signs and get a better understanding of God himself.

Notice that God is not talking about belief in this verse. He's not asking us to believe that his creation is full of his signs. He's asking us to go look and see for ourselves. This is an invitation to investigate, discover, and understand. The verse says that these signs are for a people who think. They are not for a people who just believe without bothering to think. They are for those who exercise their minds, those who reflect in their hearts, and those who use their intelligence to find causes and connections and patterns. These signs are for people who make an effort to look so that they might see.

So God says in this verse that we should take a look at what he's created and get to know him. In the heavens and the earth, in the night and the day, in the water and clouds and winds, in the animals and people and ships that sail on the sea, we can discover signs of his power, his will, his creativity, his thoughtfulness, his care. And that by observing, studying, reflecting, investigating, thinking deeply, thinking hard about these things, we are given insights, hints, and clues into the creator's creative process. And this is not just passive insight, but a chance to actively participate in his process and be his ambassadors on earth.

God, who is the greatest teacher, knows we can't learn everything through lectures. He knows we learn best what we experience tangibly and vividly. What better way to learn than to give us an experience of total immersion in the physical world? By giving us a physical body, God thrusts us into the world, into matter, into the stream of history and time. And it is through our immersion here that we are able to interact and engage with God's creation and absorb the beauty and wisdom of God that is hiding inside every little thing.

So how exactly do you learn to read the signs of God? The first step is to understand the proper relationship between the world and God, between the signs and what they signify. God is not like the gods of mythology. He is not a god like the Greek god Zeus or the Norse god Odin or the Indian god Indra. God is not like any person or thing or force in all of creation. He is not an object among other objects. He is the creative space in which all objects come and go. He is not an individual among other individuals. He is the creative ground upon which all individuals depend. He is not a being among other beings. He is the Being of all beings.

Look at the letters you're reading right now in this book. These are objects in the foreground. They appear on top of a background. Each letter, each word, and each sentence draws your attention not only to itself but also to the background from which it comes and on which it depends. Similarly, every person, every thing, and every force dwells in the foreground of creation. And yet they are all supported by the background that has created them. In this way, every creation is a sign that signifies the creator from which it comes.

The background can't appear as an object in the foreground. The background always remains the background. That's why God does not appear under your microscope or through your telescope or at the tip of your paintbrush or on the edge of your piano keys. God is not an object in the world that you can locate and manipulate. He is the creative space in which all the worlds come and go. Once you see his signs and recognize his patterns, however, you can let them give you a deeper appreciation of how he thinks. And then you can let that help you remember and feel his presence in the being that you are.

The second step is to understand that the one creator created one creation. That means you look with an eye that sees creation as one, the world as one, and life as one—without any divisions. Since God has made every single thing, he has touched it with his names and qualities. His hands are all over it. The sheer presence of a thing bears a certain signature, a fingerprint, a watermark of his involvement. The structure of a thing reveals his design. The beauty of a thing reveals his artistry. The relationship of a thing to other things in a vast web of relationships reveals his patterns. In this way, you can recognize the oneness that lives across all things because they are made by one creator.

As a direct result of this oneness, reading the signs of God can happen anywhere and at any time. In any field or endeavor, look for the signs of God. Try to see God operating in it. Whether it's literature or law, engineering or medicine, education or business, art or theater, God is there. So there really is no difference between the religious life and the worldly life. If you see a separation, you're seeing an illusion. God is everywhere. He created both heaven and earth, day and night, religion and world. God is as much in the market place, the art studio, and the science lab as he is in the prayer hall. So there is no need to think that religion stops when you leave your prayers and enter the world.

You can bring an attitude of prayer and service with you into your daily work, into your career, into your education, into your business. You can bring the qualities of presence, wonder, beauty, and gratitude into your interaction with the world, with life, and with the universe at large. You can bring the values of generosity, helpfulness, and service into your interaction with all people and cultures. All this will help you see the signs of God in the world and feel the involvement of God in your work.

Every thing, every force, and every creature is a sign that God is involved in the moving of the world. The foreground needs the background from which it came. Without his involvement, no one could live and nothing could happen. The earth is a book that tells you something about the one who made everything. You are meant to read his book so you can learn how to study his signs. You are literally surrounded by the artworks and science experiments of God. That's why art and science can become tools to help you improve your understanding of God. They can become instruments of prayer itself.

Work on changing your insides by learning that you are immersed in a world full of the wondrous signs of God. He didn't just want to tell you about them; he wanted to show you. By making you a human being on earth, God is showing you in a vivid and exhilarating way how he thinks and works. So look at his creation and see his signs. Read them, study them, go down into their depths. Every sign points to what it signifies. If you follow the signs of God, he will lead you to a better understanding of himself. Why else would he sign every atom in creation with his names and qualities? He wants to be known; he wants to be found.

DECLARE

I read the book of God.
I study the signs of God.

14

BE KIND

*Be kind
to your parents and family,
and to the orphans and the needy,
and to neighbors and travelers and servants.
Surely, God doesn't love
those who are proud and boastful.*

(Quran 4:36)

Can you name three people in your life who have been the most kind to you? Is it your mother or father, your sister or brother, a close friend, a teacher, or even a stranger? What did they do for you? How do you feel when you remember them?

Some of us can name several people in our lives who stand out as shining examples of kindness.

Their involvement in our lives helped to make us who we are. And even to this day we can't help remembering what they did without stopping for a moment and honoring the memory of their kindness. There is something holy about touching a life for the better and planting a seed for more kindness to grow in the future.

On the other hand, we can also name several people in our lives who were unkind to us. They left a wound in our minds and hearts and bodies that never quite healed. Even after all this time, it is still there and it still hurts. And the memory of how we received the wound gives us quite a bit of disappointment and grief whenever we happen to think about it. All this goes to show that kindness or the lack of it makes an impact that lasts for years.

This verse calls us to be kind to everyone: parents, family, strangers, orphans, neighbors, travelers, servants, and the needy. We are called to be kind to those we know and those we don't know, to those who are near and those who are far. We are not called to be kind because it's a nice thing to do. We are called to be kind because it embodies and extends the kindness of God.

God is kind to everyone. In fact, God made everyone and everything out of kindness. Kindness is the glue of the universe. It binds electrons and protons, parents and children, the helpful and the needy, and stars and galaxies together. Nothing can live, learn, and thrive in the web of relationships that is creation itself without kindness at its core.

God's kindness comes from two of his names, the Caring (Arabic: *al-Rahman*) and the Compassionate (Arabic: *al-Rahim*). To be caring means to be kind, to help, to nurture, and to protect. To be compassionate also means to be kind, to show mercy, to ease difficulties, and to remove suffering. When God made us out of kindness, he put little gifts from these names inside us. He weaved caring and compassion into the very beings that we are. That's why he calls us to be kind to everyone and exclude no one. Only then can we represent and embody the values of caring and compassion as his ambassadors on earth. As God stretches his kindness out to us, he calls us to stretch our kindness out to all of his creatures.

So what exactly does it mean to be kind? It means to recognize that the person in front of you is a being from God, good and beautiful and forever, just like you. It means to affirm that God has brought both of you together as members of the same family and fellow ambassadors of God in training. And out of that recognition, it means to look at that person like you are looking at a blessing. It means to listen to that person like you are receiving a gift. It means to search for the best way to serve that person in that moment, even if it is only with a smile or a glass of water.

Once upon a time, for example, the Prophet Muhammad used to take a walk down a particular street. An old woman who lived on that street would throw her trash on his head as he walked by.

He would say nothing and keep walking. Every time he walked down that street, she would throw more trash on his head. One day, as he walked down that same street, he noticed that no one threw trash on him. He asked around about the old woman and learned that she is lying sick in bed. He went to her home, found her suffering in her illness, and brought her a glass of water. He sat with her and listened to her. The old woman told him that she had misjudged him and she regretted being unkind to him. She never threw trash on anyone ever again.

This is a simple story that is often told to children, but we all need to hear it. Even though the old woman was unkind to him, the Prophet visited her during her illness because he felt compassion for her. This is what kindness does: it responds to unkindness with kindness. Some of us would have too much resentment toward the old woman to go visit her. How could the Prophet have done what he did? He remembered who he is, why he is here, and what he has been given to give to others.

If we want to be kind like the Prophet, we can't just make a wishful intention to be kind and hope it works out. Not only do we have to start practicing kindness in large and small ways, we have to find all the traces of unkindness still hiding inside us. We have to find out why we are so easily and so often unkind to each other and then turn it around. Let's look at a few examples.

First, we are unkind because we reserve kindness only for those who are like us and not for those who are different from us. To turn this around, we have to recognize that showing kindness to some people and ignoring everyone else is selective kindness. God is not selective. He is kind to every single one of his creatures. We can make a decision to develop that same vision and practice of being kind to everyone.

Second, we are unkind because we are hurting. We refuse to show kindness as a way to get back at someone who doesn't seem to be hurting. We hurt them so they can join us in the pain. To turn this around, we have to refuse to create more suffering. Hurting the other person is not going to give us relief. We can make a decision to stop the vicious circle of giving and receiving pain.

Third, we are unkind to others because we are unkind to ourselves. If we judge ourselves harshly and refuse to be compassionate, we will judge others in the same way. If we don't deserve it, why should they deserve it? To turn this around, we have to start being kind to ourselves. If God cares for us and has compassion for us, then we have to practice that same care and compassion toward ourselves. We can make a decision to share and extend that kindness to other people.

Fourth, we are unkind because we believe that acting nice is the same thing as being kind. When we act nice, we are trying to get something from someone. We act polite only to win social favors. To turn this around, we have to recognize that being kind means serving the greatest needs of the person in front of us. We can make a decision to share the gifts of God freely without expecting anything in return.

Finally, we are unkind because we only act kind when we are in the mood. A good day inspires us to show kindness while a bad day makes us irritable and impatient with other people. To turn this around, we have to recognize that kindness is not a feeling or a mood that comes and goes based on circumstances. By putting kindness in us, God made sure it would always be available to be shared. We can make a decision not to let our moods and feelings interrupt how often we practice kindness.

In this way, you can turn around every temptation to be unkind by making a deliberate decision to be kind. God made us to live together and take care of each other. Caring for any one of us benefits all of us and hurting any one of us hurts all of us. That's why none of our relationships in creation can live and thrive without kindness at their core.

Work on changing your insides by learning that you are called to be kind to everyone. Every act of kindness that you perform is both a remembrance of who you are and a recognition of who made you. When you are kind, you let the kindness of God flow from him to you and through you into the world. You become a medium for that kindness to take tangible form and bless all creatures. This is how you acknowledge and give thanks to the creator who has always been most kind to you. This is how you affirm and express that unbreakable bond that you share with all other beings. So be kind to everyone and exclude no one. They are worth it and they are worthy of it—and that includes you.

DECLARE

God is kind to everyone.
I am kind to everyone.

15

BE GENEROUS

Those who share their wealth
by night and day,
privately and publicly,
surely their reward is with their Lord.
They will have nothing
to fear or grieve.

(Quran 2:274)

Who was the first person to teach you about money? Did they manage it well or did they struggle with it? Did they use their money to help others or did they keep it to themselves? What do you think and feel today when the subject of giving money to others comes up?

If the people who taught us about money were generous with their money, we might find it a little easier to be generous as well. If they didn't feel the need to give their money to the needy, we might cling to our money tightly as well. If they struggled with money, we might feel that there is never enough money to go around as well.

At some point, we might even come to believe that the money we have earned belongs to us alone and doesn't need to be shared with anyone. In one of our more possessive moments, we might even say, "This is my money. I earned it. I put in the blood, sweat, and tears to get it. If I want to pile it up and set it on fire, I will. So don't tell me what to do with my money."

This common story of success puts our personal effort at the center. It makes us think that we alone are the authors of our success, but this is simply not true. Effort is the cup that receives God's grace. It is an important part of our success, but it is not the cause of our success. The ability and the opportunity to even make an effort comes from the mercy of God. He is the sole author and cause of our success.

For example, we wake up in the morning to fresh air blowing, birds singing, and rays of sunlight coming through the window. We make breakfast with eggs from chickens and bread from a local bakery. We put on clothes tailored and sewn by many different people. We walk down a street made by civil engineers and maintained by city workers. We use special tools for our work that were researched, built, and mass produced by a host of different companies. Millions of atoms and neurons in our brains work together just so we can think a single thought. Skin, bone, muscle, and nerve cells all move in unison just so we can pick up a pen and sign our name.

As we can see, that success story of personal effort alone has left out quite a few important details. It doesn't take into account the countless number of elements, forces, creatures, and people that have to be orchestrated just so we can have a productive day to make our efforts. And who is orchestrating this whole affair? There is no conductor of this orchestra except God.

When we say that we are putting in the blood, sweat, and tears, God is the one who gives us a heart that pumps blood and a body that produces sweat and eyes that produce tears. He grants us blessings and gifts, favors and rewards, from a wide range of his creation. He powers our efforts. He gives us the right opportunities to learn and grow. Every effort we make depends entirely on the grace of God and the contributions of all of creation, so we have to adjust our story of success accordingly. Not only do we need to include the role of God and his creation, we need to add the importance of sharing the rewards of our success with others.

This verse calls us to share our wealth with everyone, night and day, privately and publicly, for the benefit of all. As we have already seen, we don't live in isolation. We live in a web of relationships with God, people, the earth, and all of its creatures.

Since they contribute to whatever effort we make, they have a share in whatever reward we receive. In other words, we are all involved to some degree in all of creation's efforts and rewards. This is another crucial detail that the success story of personal effort conveniently leaves out.

It is easy to think that we are entitled to all of the rewards we receive for our efforts, but this is simply not true. We are never working just for ourselves. We are always working for the creator as well as the creation. That's why we don't really own our wealth. That money in our pockets is not really ours. It belongs to God. It is given to us as a trust. And now he calls us to fulfill that trust by sharing our wealth in the ways that honor God.

The first way is an acknowledgement to God that we understand that our money comes from him. We do this by giving back to God a percentage of the money that he has given us, like the prophets did before us. When the prophet Abraham gave 10% of his gains, Melchizedek, the priest-king of Salem, blessed him. This is known as the *tithe*, which means "a tenth." When the early Muslims gave 2.5% of their gains, Prophet Muhammad blessed them. This is known as the *zakat*, which means something that purifies.

These are historical examples, but they point to a principle: some percentage of our wealth must be given back to God. Not only does this bless us, it also purifies the rest of the money we have. This giving is not charity. This is an acknowledgement

REMEMBER WHO YOU ARE • 105

that God is the source of our wealth. And we demonstrate that we understand this by immediately giving a percentage of the money we receive back to God.

For example, if you receive $10 in your hand and your chosen percentage is 10%, then $1 should immediately go to God before you think about doing anything with the other nine dollars. As you send off that $1, you can say to God, "I am sending this back to you because I acknowledge that you are the source of my wealth. This money doesn't belong to me. It was given to me to give back to you. So thank you for entrusting me with this money. I enjoy fulfilling the trust you have put in me."

Think and pray and ask God for guidance in picking a percentage that feels right and generous for your life right here and right now. And pick who might receive your support. If you are an active member of a masjid, church, synagogue, temple, or another place of worship, you might consider giving them your acknowledgement money. If you don't have any strong ties to such communities, you might consider giving it to anyone who supports you in your religious and spiritual life. Begin this practice as soon as you can.

The second way is giving money to help our fellow human beings or our fellow creatures in creation. This is charitable giving. We use a percentage of our money to support those in need and those doing good in the world. There are those who are struggling for food, shelter, safety, medicine, and other basic human or animal rights. God gives us money so we can participate in helping them. It is the generosity of our donation that will provide them with the means to overcome their struggles. So we send whatever we can to them. No amount is too little and every little bit matters. If we are able to contribute the wealth of our time, knowledge, skills, and presence, we do that as well. But we must not neglect to contribute the wealth of our money.

These two noble practices bind our livelihood and our work in the world with God's work. We are not here to hoard our wealth; we are here to share our wealth. We are here to use our wealth for the benefit of all. Even God doesn't hoard his wealth, but gives it away in the form of countless upon countless blessings and gifts to all of his creatures every single second. The sun gives away light and heat in all directions every hour of the day and night. The birds give away their songs. The flowers give away their fragrance. The angels give away their help and support. So when we receive these gifts and rewards from God, we too must give them away to the rest of creation.

Work on changing your insides by learning that your wealth is a loan from God. He gives it to you to give to others. One portion is an acknowledgment to God and another portion is a charity to your sisters and brothers. Since God is a giver and you come from him, you are a giver as well. You live inside the circle of giving that flows between the creator and all his creatures. You don't give because it's a nice thing to do; you give because you are helping God take care of his creation. So share your wealth generously. Give what you are given to give. And take your place in this circle. You are most welcome here.

DECLARE

My wealth is a blessing from God.
I share my wealth for the benefit of all.

16

BE PATIENT AND FORGIVING

And whoever is patient and forgives:
that is surely the most noble thing to do.

(Quran 42:43)

Can you think of someone who has deeply hurt
you? You were close once, but their behavior
got worse and worse. Now whenever you see them,
they remind you of what happened and it stings.
You relive the hurt over and over again. It irritates
you that you still have to see them. Nothing they
say or do is right. Not only do you lose your patience with them, you find yourself having a hard
time forgiving them.

You're not alone. It's not possible to live our
lives on earth without deeply hurting someone or

being deeply hurt by someone. When we try to recall all the people that have hurt us, we might have quite a few names come up. We may not clearly remember many moments of happiness, but we seem to vividly remember quite a few moments of being misunderstood, ignored, insulted, marginalized, demeaned, betrayed, and attacked.

Getting hurt is part of our human experience. We are not made of unbreakable steel. Both women and men are made of soft skin, supple muscles, flexible minds, and sensitive hearts. In our interactions with each other and the world, we can't have pleasurable experiences without painful ones as well. Sometimes we are flexible and resilient enough to handle a difficult encounter with grace. Other times we are not able to withstand it fully. It pierces our skin, strains our muscles, overwhelms our minds, and breaks our hearts. Even though we might be stricken with pain and grief, God asks us not to strike back.

This verse calls us to be patient and forgiving in the face of hurtful experiences. In the heat of the moment, however, you might not remember to do this. When someone hurts you, you will want to hurt them back. You might not actually do it, but you will feel angry enough to consider it. You might let the pain give rise to anger and then let the anger give rise to rage. The thought of revenge tastes sweet, so you might strike back with your words or your attitudes or your actions. You want them to know that they made a big mistake when they de-

cided to hurt you. But none of us can live together
and thrive while this cycle of returning hurt for
hurt goes on. Revenge is a fire that will burn you
first before it burns anyone else. That is why God
recommends patience and forgiveness.

This has little to do with our typical understanding of "forgive and forget." When someone hurts
you and you try to forgive them and forget it happened, you could still walk away from the encounter
resenting that person. You could still be surprised,
shocked, and angry that they hurt you. You could
still carry it and let it fester for days, weeks, months,
and even years. If you are able, you might avoid
that person. If you are not able, you might smile,
make small talk, and act like nothing is wrong. You
can only do this if you numb yourself, pretend that
you are not hurt, and deny that anything ever happened. All this might make you think that you have
forgiven them and forgotten about it. But the hurtful event and the memory of how it all happened is
still there, right beneath the skin, waiting to erupt
into your awareness, as raw pain and grief and dis-
belief. Forgiving and forgetting by suppressing the
truth and going numb can't help us live together
and thrive either.

So what does it mean to be patient and forgiving? To be patient means to remember who you are.
If you think of yourself as a body that can be broken, a mind that can be offended, and a heart that
can be hurt, the whole world will feel prickly and
dangerous. If you think of yourself as a being from

God, you can know that who you really are can't be hurt by anyone's words or actions. Your mind can be surprised and stunned. Your heart can feel shocked and betrayed. But the being that you are can't be harmed at all. It can't be broken, offended, or hurt by any attack whatsoever. This unshakeable foundation is the source of your true patience. To be patient, then, is to release yourself from the idea that you are the victim.

Of course, this doesn't mean that you do nothing while you get insulted, mistreated, and attacked. You remember your true identity and you lean on God to show you the next step. Then you can use the strength, wisdom, and courage you receive from God to respond to the attack. Sometimes the response is raising your sword and shield and disarming your attacker. Sometimes the response is running and getting out of the situation. Sometimes the response is using the law of the land to defend your rights. Sometimes the response is using your words to bring truth, clarity, and kindness to the situation. Sometimes the response is turning the other cheek. Sometimes the response is just silence and prayer. When you remember that you belong to God, you have a lot more ways to respond than taking revenge or going numb.

If being patient means to remember who *you* are, then being forgiving means to remember who *they* are. Forgiveness doesn't mean to recall in exact detail all the ways that someone hurt you and then decide that you are willing to forget about it.

Forgiveness is actually the willingness to see the other person as a being from God too. It is a shift in focus from their behavior to their true identity. Underneath the drama of their hurtful attacks, this is your sister or brother in the family of beings. They are good and beautiful, just like you. They may not talk like it right now. They may not act like it right now. But sooner or later, they will. It is not your task to change their minds or free them from their own suffering. But it is your task to hold a vision of their true identity and look for opportunities to reconcile. To be forgiving, then, is to release yourself from the idea that they are the victimizer.

So how do you practice patience and forgiveness? Make a list of every single person who has hurt you in your life, whether they are physically alive or not. What names and faces come to mind? Write their names down. Speak the name of the first person on your list and say the following to them, as if they were standing in front of you:

"You are a being from God, just like me. You are good and beautiful, just like me. God made us together and brought us here together. Yes, hurtful things were said and hurtful things were done. But even in the worst moments, the beings that God made us were never harmed. As God is patient and forgiving with me, I am ready to be patient and forgiving with you. I am ready to see you only as God sees you. I am ready to heal in my mind and heart all that was said and done. I forgive you. I release you. God bless you. Peace be upon you."

Take a moment to let that sink in. And then move on to the next name. Spend the next few hours, days, and weeks to practice this with every single person on the list. Take a break when you need to and come back to the list. When you get to the bottom of the list, start again with the first name at the top and repeat the practice even more intentionally and sincerely. Go through all the names on the list as often as you need to. You will know that you have forgiven a person when thinking of them as a beautiful being from God interests you more than thinking of them as someone who hurt you.

Once you learn what forgiveness feels like when you give it, you will be drawn to find out what it feels like when you receive it. So make a list of every single person you have hurt in your life, whether they are physically alive or not. Go through all the names on the list and ask them to be patient and forgiving with you. If you are able to meet anyone from the list in person, meet with them and ask them to forgive you.

Work on changing your insides by learning that God calls us to be patient and forgiving. This looks less like "forgive and forget" and more like "remember and reconcile." People are going to hurt you and you are going to hurt them. But if you practice patience and forgiveness with each other, you can both overcome the hurt and restore the relationship. And then it will be clear to both of you that recognizing the humanity of all the people involved is far more important than keeping a record of the hurtfulness. A tear can be sewn again. A broken bone can be mended again. A people in conflict can be reconciled again. So be patient and forgiving and help God bring your family back together again.

DECLARE

No one can hurt what I really am.
I am patient and forgiving with everyone.

17

BE A STUDENT

Say: "My Lord, increase me in knowledge."

(Quran 20:114)

When we grow up inside a religious tradition, we are told to put our faith in a set of beliefs, follow a list of rules, and participate in an array of rituals that mark the stages of a life from birth to death. The main work of our religious lives on earth is to force ourselves to believe in those beliefs as an act of pure will. If we are able to keep believing in this way while fighting off every doubt, God will be pleased with us and allow us to enter heaven in the afterlife—all because we kept the faith.

Of course, thinking too much about those beliefs, rules, and rituals, especially to the point of questioning them, would hurt our chances of getting into heaven. So we are allowed to think and question only for the purpose of fully adopting those beliefs. We are not allowed to get creative, experiment, and take risks. Like a fortress of belief, the tradition uses faith as a shield against any knowledge that would disturb the tradition itself. This seems to offer us a bit of comfort and reassurance, but only by keeping us in the dark. We go along with all this because our family and community are going along with it.

And then one day we leave our family and community. We move farther away to study in school or to start a new life in another city. We meet all kinds of different people. They practice other faiths as well as no faith. We even meet some people who practice different versions of our own faith. And we learn that there are many ways to practice religion that may not look anything like the one we were raised with. In this new place, we have the freedom to think and question as much as we want. No one is going to stop us.

Some of us take full advantage of this situation. We think the hard thoughts and raise the hard questions, but the results are not so pleasant. The limitations of our family's religious tradition become painfully apparent. We realize that some of the beliefs we were taught to believe don't make sense anymore. The rules we were told to follow are too rigid. The rituals we were told to practice feel dry and lifeless. The God we were told to please seems so far away. Now that we know more, we believe less. Knowledge has woken us up from a faith that had only put us to sleep. It's a whole new world for us. And yet something is still missing.

What we don't initially realize is that we have simply reversed our prejudices. We used to be on the side of faith and we looked down on those who had abandoned faith in their search for knowledge. Now we are on the side of knowledge and we look down on those who are walking by faith. By regarding faith and knowledge as enemies who are always separated from each other, we have split our understanding into two. But what if this easy separation of faith and knowledge, practiced by both religious and scientific communities, is too easy. What if faith and knowledge are not actually enemies, but friends working together toward a common goal?

This verse invites us to ask God to increase our knowledge. Now what do people of faith do with a verse like this? Shouldn't it say, "Increase me in faith"? And yet it says, "Increase me in knowledge." When God brought us into being, he gave us a little gift from his name, "the Knowing" (Arabic: al-Alim). This is what allows us to know, to be aware, and to understand. To reach for more knowledge, we not only have to use our previous knowledge, we also have to use our faith to explore the unknown and make new discoveries. In this way, faith and knowledge work more closely together than we ever realized. Let me explain.

Faith is a starting point, a beginning of a search, a preliminary step in an investigation, the initial phase of an exploration. It all starts with a hint, a clue, a story, a sign, a seed, an intuition, a feeling, a dream, or a vision. You have faith that this initial seed is important and valuable. You have faith that the path it takes you down will lead to something even more important and valuable. And while you are on this path, you think and rethink, you learn and unlearn, you encounter and interact, you test and retest. You try and fail and try again. You collect experiences. You connect the dots. You outline the patterns. And you finally begin to understand and increase in knowledge.

That initial seed of faith might turn out to be true or false, useful or useless, practical or impractical. Either way, this seed bursts open and generates other seeds that branch out in many directions and form the trees of your explorations. Your knowledge is based on the fullness of those trees. Faith is not a seed you grip tightly in your hand and hope that God will reward you one day for the tightness of your grip. Faith is a seed you plant and water so it can grow into a forest of knowledge. Faith is not an end in itself, but an essential part of the entire enterprise of seeking, collecting, sharing, and extending knowledge.

So what is the best way to ask God to increase you in knowledge? First, always think of yourself as a student of God. No matter how old you are, no matter how much you already know, and no matter how much you have already accomplished, always be a student. Increase your curiosity about everything. Study yourself. Study people. Study all of creation.

Travel the world and meet your fellow beings from God. Listen to their stories. Learn their languages. Read books from a wide variety of subjects. Write in the margins. Take notes. Keep journals. Engage the material you are learning. Carry a backpack as a reminder that you are always a student.

Second, widen your concept of knowledge. Knowledge is more than just the facts that everyone can agree on. It includes awareness, experience, perception, and imagination. Knowledge isn't just math and science. It is also art, literature, psychology, philosophy, history, law, politics, and many others. It is knowledge of yourself. It is knowledge of people and cultures and the world. It is knowledge of the signs and names of God as they are reflected inside ourselves and across all of creation. So cast your net widely and embrace the humanities and the sciences and all the connective tissues in between.

Third, teach what you know. Now that you've gained some knowledge, it's time to share it. Hoarding knowledge to help you feel clever and superior over others is a sickness of the mind and heart. Knowledge, like every other form of wealth, is a loan you borrow from God. It is not meant to be enjoyed privately, but shared with all of creation. In fact, teaching is the best way to deepen and refine what you think you already know. A good teacher is nothing less than a good student with a burning desire to share.

Fourth, make knowledge a core part of your religious tradition. It could encourage both faith and knowledge with faith as the first step and knowledge as the end goal. It could make space for raising questions, searching for answers, making mistakes, asking better questions, and trying again. It could support its members in using beliefs, rules, and rituals in far more personal and creative ways. And it could do all this in an open-minded and large-hearted manner so that the tradition evolves as the members evolve. Such a tradition looks less like a "fortress of belief" and more like a "school of knowledge."

Finally, pursue the knowledge of first things first. There is no end to what you can know, but your time is precious. So focus first and foremost on knowing the things that are closest to you, the things that last, the things that matter. Get to know who you are. Get to know who people are. Get to know who God is. On these three timeless pieces of knowledge, you can build a strong, joyful, creative, and compassionate life. Make a personal effort to make these three your priority. Don't wait until your later years to do this. Start pursuing these three immediately so your knowledge of them can be a foundation for you for the rest of your life.

Work on changing your insides by learning that God wants to increase you in knowledge. Let your faith inspire you to seek and find knowledge, so that you actually become knowledgeable and not remain merely faithful. The more you know, the more intelligently, compassionately, and creatively you can serve God and all of creation. Keep asking questions. Keep answering your questions. Keep questioning your answers. Keep asking new questions. This spiral of learning never ends. You never arrive at a place where you can stop learning. There are always and forever new and exciting things to explore and discover. So keep turning over the leaves. Keep peeling back the layers. Keep diving deeper and deeper into the countless signs and endless names of God.

DECLARE

I am a student of God.
I share my knowledge for the benefit of all.

18

BE AN ARTIST

*Don't you see
that God has given you
every single thing
in the heavens and the earth,
and has made you abundant
with inner and outer gifts?*

(Quran 31:20)

When you hear the word "artist," what kind of person comes to mind? Is it a painter or a sculptor? Is it someone who draws or makes sketches? Is it a musician or a singer or a dancer? Is it an actor or a filmmaker or a photographer? Is it a novelist or a poet? What exactly is an artist?

Some people will tell you that an artist can only be someone who works in these specific fields of the fine arts. Such a person produces works of art that fill the museums, art galleries, and symphony halls of the world. Everyone else, even when they might be an expert in their field or a craftsperson, is not a real artist.

This understanding of art and the artist is typical, but it is also mistaken. It sees art as an activity that is separate from every other type of work. It identifies only a few people as having the necessary talents and skills to practice art. It looks to a certain class of wealthy and influential individuals who define for everyone else the nature and character of art. All of this, however, doesn't actually define art. It merely describes a particularly narrow and exclusive understanding of art in modern societies.

Older societies, on the other hand, had a much broader understanding of art and the artist. They understood that art can't be separated from the rest of life as a distinct activity. Life is a work of art. Everyone who participates in life can practice art. Living and working require daily acts of creativity. All people are gifted with artistic abilities, not just a few individuals who are recognized by the wealthy as proper artists. Art can show up in anything people think or say or do. That's why it can never be limited to the fields of the fine arts alone. It is available to anyone to practice and perform anywhere and anytime.

This verse says that God has given us all kinds of gifts: hidden and manifest, implicit and explicit, potential and actual, inner and outer. By giving us all these gifts, God equips us to participate in the creative activity that drives all of creation. He teaches us how to draw these gifts down from their intangible source, press them into their tangible forms, and share them with all of creation. When we combine, mix, and blend these gifts, we help God reveal, unfold, and extend his creation. This is what makes life a work of art. This is what makes all of us artists.

When God spoke us into being, he gave us a little gift from his name, "the Designer" (Arabic: *al-Musawwir*). We are all artists because we come from the Artist. He put the desire to practice our art and create something new at our core. We are drawn to make things and remake them. We are drawn to touch things and reshape them. We are drawn to imagine things and redesign them. In this way, God has made every single woman, man, and child on earth an artist—and that includes you.

So how can you begin to be the artist God made you to be? The first step is to take ownership of your role as an artist of God. Accept and acknowledge that you have been given countless inner and outer gifts. Accept and acknowledge that God is inviting you to help him extend his creation through your works of art. If you think that other people are gifted while you have been left empty-handed, then you are hiding from your own gifts. If you think that other people have much to contribute while you have almost nothing, then you are hiding your gifts from others. You are an artist of God; own it.

The second step is to explore your gifts with God. Find out exactly what gifts, talents, and skills he has given you. These gifts may have been delivered to your house, but they might still be sitting outside your door. Or maybe you took them inside, put them in a closet, and never opened them. The time has come for you to fully unwrap, open, and enjoy these gifts.

Carve out time every day for your creative life: 20 minutes, 30 minutes, an hour. Don't wait for your family and work commitments to become easier and less busy before you carve out this holy time. Identify a space in your home and go there consistently during this time to explore your gifts. This will give your mind and heart and body a clear signal that you are ready to practice your art with God.

In this creative time and space, you can read, write, pray, reflect, journal, draw, sketch, make, craft, code, design, build, paint, sing, dance, and play. You can scream and shout. You can laugh and cry. You can tell God your stories, jokes, and deepest secrets. You can listen to God tell you his stories, jokes, and deepest secrets. You can sit in silence and just be. In this way, you can receive more fully and make good art with all those ideas, intuitions, and inspirations that God is always pouring into you.

So let yourself think open-minded thoughts and feel large-hearted feelings. Be creative with your remembrance, thankfulness, and studies. Be imaginative in how you practice kindness, generosity, patience, and forgiveness. Don't be embarrassed or afraid to explore your gifts. Ask God to show them to you and teach you about them and explore them with you.

The third step is to design your life like an artist. Does your life support your role as an artist of God? What changes do you need to make so you can share your gifts more easily with the world? An artist is both spontaneous and intentional; she is both imaginative and methodical. How can you better structure your days, weeks, months, and years so that they support your art, your career, and your family? You never have to choose one or the other. Ask God for help, use your imagination, and find a way.

This is the time for you to put down your fears and be brave. What are the things you always wanted to do in your life but you still haven't been able to do them? Maybe you were too afraid to do them. Maybe you didn't know how to do them. Maybe you didn't have enough resources or support to do them. Whatever the reason might be, this is the time for you to do them. You are never too old and it is never too late to give birth to the dreams God has put in you. So be brave and begin today.

The fourth step is to share your gifts. As much as exploring and enjoying your gifts will enrich you, you can't imagine how much sharing them will enrich other people. Your gifts are not yours alone.

God gave them to you to give to others. Don't say, "Who am I stand up in the crowd and act like I have something to share? Who am I to pretend I have something to offer?" You are an artist of God. He sent you here to help people with your gifts. You are not doing this for fame and fortune; you are doing this in service and devotion to God.

While you are helping people with your gifts, you are helping the world as well. Every society around the world has its struggles and challenges. More often than not, these can't be addressed by the same type of thinking from the past. They can only be addressed by a different kind of thinking that can imagine a better future. By contributing your gifts as an artist of God, you can help your society see what it hasn't seen or has been unwilling to see. You can help your society hear what it hasn't heard or has been unwilling to hear. You can help your society learn what it hasn't learned or has been unwilling to learn. In this way, you can help your society overcome the gaps, blindspots, and limitations of its own perceptions and decisions. You can help your society grow and evolve toward a better future where the well-being of every woman, man, and child is protected and celebrated.

Work on changing your insides by learning that God has given you countless inner and outer gifts. Your life is a work of art being worked on together by you and God. Your part is to receive these gifts, unfold them, and share them for the benefit of all. God's part is to spread them out so they help your society keep growing and evolving. So bring forth your creativity and artistry. Bring forth your unique gifts and perspectives. Bring forth the brilliance you have gathered from your accomplishments and the wisdom you have gained from your mistakes. Give what God gave you to give. Be the artist God made you to be. Serve the world artfully. After all, there are people you've never met waiting to receive the blessings of your gifts.

DECLARE

I am an artist of God.
I practice my art for the benefit of all.

19

BE A PARTNER

And we created you in pairs.

(Quran 78:8)

Have you ever felt that the world was too big to explore by yourself? Have you ever wished you had someone to share your life with? Have you ever wanted to go through the ups and downs of life with another person by your side?

There's a reason you feel that. It's not because nature is telling you to find a mate and have children. It's not because society is telling you to settle down after you've reached a certain age. It's not because all your friends are doing it and you feel like you need to catch up. It's because God made us to live, learn, and grow in pairs.

This verse says that God created us in pairs. In fact, God made many things in pairs: day and night, light and dark, up and down, right and left, even and odd, inner and outer, hidden and manifest, potential and actual, intention and action, theory and practice, mind and heart, and so on. Some of the most important pairs in life look like this: mother and daughter, mother and son, father and daughter, father and son, brother and sister, grandparent and grandchild, teacher and student, friend and friend, and so on.

One of the most remarkable pairs is partner and partner. Sometimes this is when two human beings have chosen each other to be the person with whom they want to build a life. They choose to live together, to learn from each other, to share their joys and sorrows, and to grow in their minds and hearts. Other times this is when two friends have chosen each other to be companions in life, without any romantic involvement.

The mind was made to work with another mind. The heart was made to join with another heart. When this doesn't happen, the mind closes and the heart narrows. The mind draws a comfortable circle around itself and refuses to go outside of it. Why should it? There is no one around to challenge it. The heart too withdraws into its own chambers. It might still care about a few people, but it will add no more to its list of affections. Why should it? There is no one around to bring it out of hiding. The mind and heart think they are finished growing. In a living partnership, however, there is no such thing as being finished because mutual growth is always happening. It has no end.

Some of the images we are taught about this kind of partnership is that every day is full of excitement and bliss. And then two people enter into a partnership and find that it's less wonderful and joyous than they were told. That makes them think that they are either with the wrong person or that they are not made for this kind of life or that they are just doing it wrong. In some cases, where there is no genuine affection and good will, this might be true. But in most cases, it's due to entering into a partnership without understanding its true purpose.

The purpose of a partnership is not daily bliss, but daily companionship and growth. Pleasure and joy, helpfulness and gratitude, disagreement and reconciliation, and learning and growth are all mixed in. Your partner is not there just to be your companion in life, but also to challenge you to grow in your life. And you are there to do the same for them.

For example, both of you will uncover the cuts and sores and wounds that are hidden in each other's minds and hearts: painful memories from childhood, abrasive behaviors inherited from the family that raised you, selfish habits of survival adopted as an adult, and so on. Even though these things might have helped you in the past, they can no longer serve you in the present, especially if you have a conscious and intentional relationship with your partner.

In the supportive space of the partnership, you can explore the wounds together and reach a degree of awareness and forgiveness that would not have been possible without your partner helping you through it. You are safe in feeling it, talking about it, getting a larger understanding of it, and eventually releasing it so that you are no longer burdened by it. This kind of growth can't happen as easily and quickly without a partner who brings both kindness and clarity to the situation.

And you do the same for them. You can be a listening ear and a gentle guide to your partner as they overcome the wounds in their own mind and heart. In this way, you can serve each other for the purpose of your mutual growth. This is why the most potent discoveries and opportunities to grow as a human being happen inside a partnership. In fact, all the practices involved in remembering who you are as an individual have corresponding practices in a partnership. In other words, partnership raises the same sets of questions about identity, purpose, and nourishment and addresses them to both partners.

For example, can you help each other remember who you are? When you look at her, can you remember that she is a being from God? When you see him, can you see that he is good and beautiful? Can you help each other remember that you are forever?

Can you help each other remember that you were made from a single being? Can you see that you share all the same qualities and capacities? Can you remember that you were also made different so that you might know one another? Can you use those differences to appreciate each other, rather than criticize each other? Can you remember that you are ambassadors of God? Can you remind each other that you are here to represent God's interests on earth?

Can you help each other bring your hopes and fears to God alone? Can you help each other see God as a teacher and become his students? Can you help each other see God as a friend and become his friends? Can you let God be the third in your partnership?

Can you help each other to be kind, to think about the other person, to speak to them like you want to be spoken to? Can you help each other to be generous and share your wealth with the needy? Can you help each other forgive and reconcile?

Can you help each other keep learning, keep increasing your knowledge, so that you are always students of God? Can you take turns being a student and teacher to each other? Can you nurture each other's creativity so that the artist in you can influence everything you do?

Can you commit to serving God, each other, and the world so that the benefits of your partnership is not only felt by both of you, but by everyone around you? Can you join forces so that both of you are capable of making such powerful contributions to the world that you could not make individually?

Can you see how partnership magnifies our remembrance of who we are and why we're here? Can you see how it multiplies our efforts because we are doing it together with another person?

You might be wondering, "All this is great, but what if I can't find a partner? If I can't find someone to build a life with, then what am I supposed to do?" This is a genuine concern and, as you well know, this is not something anyone can control. If you genuinely want to experience a partnership like this, ask God to help you find someone who is equally interested in the same thing and stay open to meeting them. Start by being the person God wants you to be and doing the things he wants you to do. As you walk down this path, you will meet others who are walking down the same path. And, God willing (Arabic: *inshallah*), opportunities for partnership may arise.

At the same time, don't wait for a partner to show up before you practice having intentional and meaningful relationships with people. Build your own extended family of friends, companions, cousins, nephews, nieces, neighbors, and so on. Open your heart and build a community of kindred beings whose true identity you are willing to recognize, whose true purpose you are willing to serve, and whose true nourishment you are willing to support. They are all your sisters and brothers because you all belong to that larger family of beings. And you will find that many of the qualities of partnership are available in these relationships as well.

Work on changing your insides by learning that God created us in pairs so that we live, learn, and grow together. Partnership is the practice of making the two into one. It is the remembering of the larger family of beings through the nurturing of our own smaller family of beings on earth. This life of "You are beautiful" and "I'm so happy to share this life with you" and "Let me help you with that" and "Talk to me, I'm listening" and "I'm sorry" and "Thank you" and "Don't worry, God is with us" and "You can do this, I believe in you" is a holy life. It is a blessed life. It is a gifted life. And you are invited.

DECLARE

I grow into a larger life with my partner.
I offer God a greater service with my partner.

NOW, SERVE

20

HONOR YOUR PARENTS

Your Lord has commanded
that you worship no one except him,
and that you show kindness to your parents.
Once they reach old age,
don't be irritated with them
and don't criticize them,
but speak to them
with words of respect and grace.
And pray for them by saying: "My Lord,
have mercy on them and care for them
as they cared for me when I was little."

(Quran 17:23-24)

All the great stories are stories about families. Can you recall some of the families from scripture? Eve (Arabic: *Hawa*), her husband Adam, and their children. Hagar (*Hajar*), Sarah, Abraham, and their sons Ishmael (*Ismail*) and Isaac (*Ishak*). Mary (*Maryam*) and her son Jesus (*Isa*). Khadija, her husband Muhammad, and their daughter Fatima. Their stories specifically and vividly illustrate for us the blessing and the struggle that is wrapped up in this beautiful and mysterious thing called family.

The story of your family is unique, of course, but it contains all the elements of the great stories. Every member of your family is a being from God. Every one of them enters the world with their own blessings and struggles. How they work out their gifts and challenges determines their character in the story and their role in the family. They push and pull in different directions. They take risks and make mistakes. They forget and ignore. They remember and return. This is what creates the drama and the tension in the family. And somehow, in God's infinite wisdom, this is the way you all live, learn, and grow together.

It all starts when you inherit the blessings and struggles of your mother, father, and other caregivers. Can you think of what blessings they all brought into the family? How did it affect you? What did they struggle with? Are you still struggling with those same things? Perhaps your mother was an accomplished psychologist or engineer or business owner. Now you are doing the same because she paved the way for you. Perhaps your father struggled with money and now you struggle with the same issue.

No matter how big or small they might be, these blessings and struggles imprint themselves on us. At first we are not fully aware that this has happened. Only later in life, as we learn to reflect on the past and imagine different choices that we could have made, do we begin to see the imprints from our parents. In the same way that we inherit physical characteristics from their physical bodies, we also inherit subtle patterns from their mental and emotional lives.

As we get older and find our individuality, we receive new blessings and struggles that are unique to us. We develop our own perspectives and directions in life. These often conflict with the ones we inherited from our parents. And that stirs up the drama and the tension we already have with them.

What if you don't want to become a psychologist or engineer or a business owner like your mother? Are you letting her down? Do you resent your mother for putting pressure on you? Does she look down on you for not following her path? What if you figure out how to handle your money quite well? Do you look down on your father for not figuring it out? Do you get angry at your father for all the hardships your family could have avoided if he had made different decisions?

Does all of this change the way you behave toward your parents? Is it hard to speak kindly to your parents without criticizing them? Is your mother's overbearing personality all you can see in her? Are your father's mistakes the only things you can see about him? Is your resentment toward them larger and heavier than your gratitude toward them?

This verse calls us to show kindness to our parents, to speak to them respectfully, and to pray for them. This is an invitation to build a relationship of appreciation with our parents. God wants us to treat our parents like he wants us to treat all people: with kindness, generosity, patience, and forgiveness. God doesn't want us to cling to years of resentment. He wants us to remember who our parents really are. So how do you do this?

First, recognize your parents as beings from God, good and beautiful and forever. As fellow members in the family of beings, they are your sisters and brothers. They are one with you because you share the same nature as them. They are different from you because God made them different by design. Like you, they came into the world with their own blessings and struggles and gifts and challenges. They entered the world as interesting characters in the interesting story of your family. They came to work through their story, seeing where it leads, sometimes embracing their gifts and challenges, sometimes avoiding them—just like you.

The next time you see your mother or father, look into their eyes and tell yourself: "She was a little girl once. He was a small boy once. They both laughed and played. They both had dreams and struggles." Try to stretch your compassion out to them.

Second, be grateful to your parents for all the good they did when they raised you. You were small, helpless, crying, unable to speak or do anything for yourself. And they looked past your crying and runny noses and dirty diapers and cared for you anyway, hour after hour, day after day, year after year.

You didn't come into the world looking like them, talking like them, interested in the same things as them, able to carry on enjoyable conversations with them. In other words, you were nothing like them when you got here. They were full-grown adults and you were a newborn baby. You could do nothing for them when you got here. And they cared for you anyway.

Similarly, in our adulthood, your parents may not be like you to a great or small degree, but you are asked to be kind to them, to speak gently to them, and to pray for them, asking God, "Have mercy on them as they did care for me when I was little." In other words, have mercy on them because they had mercy on me.

Third, forgive your parents for any mistakes they made. Make a decision to stop grading your parents over and over again on how well or how poorly they parented you. Forgive your parents for not being perfect parents. Forgive yourself for not being a perfect kid. Forgive your family for not being a perfect family.

You are not the victim of an imperfect childhood. No matter what was lacking in your childhood, know that God will fill whatever lack you perceive. Bring the empty and sore spots in your heart to God and let him heal them. You don't need to carry around the judgement and resentment and hurt anymore.

Forgive your parents and release them, so you can be released as well. Accept your parents as God accepts them. Accept their successes and failures as you accept your own. Give them the same space you want to be given to make your own decisions and bear the consequences.

Finally, be kind to them and pray for them. Remember that your parents came here with their own blessings and struggles. Some of those will get imprinted on you. And you will imprint your own blessings and struggles on your children. As your parents work out the story of their lives, they need your kindness and prayers to support their efforts. It doesn't mean you have to agree with them about everything. It doesn't mean you have to see the world like they do. It doesn't mean you have to live in the world like they do. What it does mean is that you are kind to them, you speak to them respectfully, and you pray for them.

And if your parents are no longer physically alive, the opportunity to practice kindness toward them is still available. Since you and your parents are beings who live forever, your relationship with them is larger than death itself. You can still send them your thoughts and feelings of kindness. Speak respectfully to your parents as if they are alive now and sitting right in front of you. Speak to them as if you were speaking to them on their birthday, wishing them well, happy for them, seeing them blow out the candles on their birthday cake. Speak to them respectfully, and pray for them. It is all seen and heard and recorded and conveyed. God does not waste even your smallest efforts of kindness.

Work on changing your insides by learning that your parents are beings from God, just like you. Their story and your story met for a few years in this beautiful and mysterious thing called family. Be grateful for the blessings and gifts they shared with you. Be patient and forgiving for the struggles and challenges they brought with them. And know that a day will come when you will communicate happily and fully with them, when all resentment and misunderstanding will be wiped away, when all are forgiven, when all are released, and when all are living joyfully in the garden of being, dining at the banquet of being, joined together in the family of being, inside the all-embracing caring and compassion of God.

DECLARE

I honor my parents with kindness.
I pray for my parents with kindness.

21

SERVE ALL WOMEN

O people!
Be careful of your duty to your Lord
who created you from a single being
and from it created its partner
and from those two has created
a multitude of women and men.
Be careful of your duty toward God
when you make claims of one another,
and toward the wombs that gave birth to you.
Surely, God is watching you.

(Quran 4:1)

Who are the most important women in your life? Is it your mother or daughter or sister or cousin? How did your father regard your mother in comparison to himself? How were you taught to see your sister in comparison to yourself? What do you think about your daughter in comparison to other little girls and boys? In other words, how do you see women in comparison to men?

No matter what country we visit, no matter what culture we explore, no matter what level of education we reach, the dominant idea among men is this: men get to rule and women get to play a role under his rule. Even nice guys carry this dominant idea. Men have conspired with each other to create a world culture that crowns men in all matters.

Men believe that they have a God-given right to rule, but that rule is the most abusive form of tyranny. Women have been the worse casualties of this tyranny because they have been prevented from exercising their own God-given rights. They have had their own opportunity to speak, influence, and lead taken away from them under the threat of violence and death.

So where did men get the idea that men are superior and women are inferior? From the lie that whispers in their own minds and hearts that they are the rulers and women are their property. From other men who are also following the lie. From the nightmare of history, which is a long brutal record of that lie. From the values and norms of a world culture built on top of the lie.

This lie says that God made a man first because men were made to lead. It says that God made a woman out of the man because women were made to serve and follow men. It claims that the superiority of men is the natural order of things as well as a commandment from God above. This is what the lie teaches, but God teaches something else altogether.

This verse says that God made the first woman and the first man out of a single being. The woman was not made out of the man. The man was not made out of the woman. Both women and men share the same nature with each other because they were created from that single being. All the blessings, gifts, names, and qualities that God gave to that single being were passed onto each and every woman and man made from that being. That's why there is no difference in the physical, mental, emotional, moral, and spiritual capacities of women and men.

This account of the creation of all human beings announces the equality of women with men, especially since they share the exact same origin. It tells us that a human being comes in two forms: woman and man. A human being is not a man who is accompanied by a lesser version of himself called a woman. They are both equal. They are not like the sun and the moon; they are both suns or they are both moons.

So what do we do with the truth of women and men being equal while living in a world culture that denies this truth? As ambassadors and artists of God, there can be only one choice in front of us: we have to serve all women by working for the equality of women everywhere. As the verse indicates, we have a duty to God to place no limits on women and men that God himself has not placed. That means we have to dismantle a world culture built on top of the lie and rebuild it on top of equality.

What can the men among us do to help? We have to transform our own minds and hearts so that we recognize all women as our equals. We have to renounce our loyalty to the lie and become fierce allies to women and their equality. We have to examine our own unexamined prejudices, biases, and fears regarding women. We have to uncover and uproot our distorted understanding of women as lesser human beings. We have to stop being the center of attention and give the stage and the spotlight to women. We have to listen to women and follow their lead. Only then can we be a part of the movement to dismantle and rebuild those values and norms of our world culture that doesn't recognize the equality of women and men everywhere.

This includes those of us who think we are nice guys just because we have never physically hurt a single woman in our lives. It's not enough to be a nice guy and still perceive women as less than men. It's not enough to be a nice guy and still let a culture that discriminates against women continue to operate, unchecked and unchallenged. Being a nice guy is not an accomplishment, but a refusal to get involved. Don't be a nice guy; be a fierce ally. Be ready and willing to stand up for equality by speaking out against every form of inequality.

When you hear other men talk about women in disrespectful ways, speak up. Don't just laugh along with your boys. Talk to them about how men can start changing the conversation they have with each other about women. Don't be a nice guy; be a fierce ally.

When members of your family talk down to your mother, your daughter, your sister, your aunt, or your niece, speak up. Ask them if the prophets Muhammad, Jesus, and Moses talked down to the women in their lives. Start a movement in your own family to speak to all women with respect and honor. Don't be a nice guy; be a fierce ally.

When your workplace gives all the men promotions and ignores the women, speak up. Talk to everyone who will listen and do everything in your power and influence to create more opportunities for women to take leadership positions. Don't be a nice guy; be a fierce ally.

When your society upholds laws that deny equal rights to women, speak up. Contribute your time, effort, and knowledge to help the appropriate organizations and movements to change those laws. Don't be a nice guy; be a fierce ally.

When your culture tries to put walls around your daughter by making her think that she is only supposed to be interested in a handful of subjects because she's a girl, speak up for her and tear down those walls. Teach her that her interests and pursuits can be as wide as the heavens and the earth and beyond. This is the spacious freedom that God himself has given to her. And no man can take that away from her, not even her own father. Don't be a nice guy; be a fierce ally.

When your culture tries to train your son to become numb to his conscience and to behave aggressively toward women as a sick and twisted attempt to feel powerful in the world, speak up for him and teach him a better way. Teach him a large-hearted definition of what it means to be a man, like the one Muhammad, Jesus, and Moses followed. Work for the equality of women by raising sons who will work for the equality of women. Don't be a nice guy; be a fierce ally.

Once you begin to serve all women in this way, you will begin to recognize who they really are. Women are powerful beings from God. They are one-half of humanity. All of God's names and qualities have been given to them as blessings and gifts. They are more than capable of leading the world, advancing knowledge and compassion, and celebrating our oneness and difference. Once women and men embrace each other as partners and allies, they can finally be healed and reconciled to one other. And once women fully reclaim their God-given rights, the world can finally be made whole again.

Work on changing your insides by learning that God made women and men equal by making them out of a single being. Men don't decide what women can be, what they can have, or what they can do. Women decide that for themselves based on what

God has already given them. And what God has given, let no man try to take away. When we perceive women as less than men, when we take power away from them, or when we make them silent and invisible, it robs us of our humanity and dignity. Only by honoring women as our equals can our full humanity be restored to us. In this way, we are called not only to champion the equality of the women in our lives, but to create a world culture that champions the equality of women everywhere.

DECLARE

God created women and men from the same being.
I work for the equality of women everywhere.

2 2

TEACH THE CHILDREN

[The Prophet Luqman says:]
O my dear son!
Pray regularly and enjoin what is good
and forbid what is not good,
and persevere no matter what happens to you:
that is surely the most noble thing to do.

(Quran 31:17)

What images come to mind when you think about children? When some people think about children, they frown. They think of selfish and noisy little people running around, screaming, getting into trouble, not listening to anyone, and making a total mess. This rowdy picture of children makes some adults think twice about having children of their own. It also makes them uncomfortable with being left alone with children. But this way of thinking about children misses all the beautiful parts of a much larger story.

When other people think about children, they smile. They think of sweet and innocent little people that have been assigned to them by God for their nurturing and growth. By caring for these children, they get to revisit childhood all over again. They get to relearn everything as they teach it to their children. They get to see the world with new eyes. This entire relationship between caregivers and children is God's brilliant strategy to help us learn how to care for each other.

This verse indicates that children need us to teach them affectionately about the truth of who they are. In this verse, we are eavesdropping on a conversation between the prophet Luqman and his son. After affectionately calling him "my dear son," Luqman points out to him the importance of prayer, doing good, and persevering through the troubles of life. Rather than letting his son figure it out on his own, he shares what he himself has found to be important. Luqman has done the work to orient his life around God, so he can teach his child from the authority of his own experience.

In the same way, all girls and boys need to learn this kind of wisdom from their mothers and fathers and caregivers. It is not enough to teach our children language and manners. It is not enough to teach them reading and writing and math and science. We must teach them the knowledge and the wisdom that comes from knowing who we are, why we are here, and what feeds us.

So how can you teach your children or the children in your extended family, like Luqman teaches his son? First, recognize that children are little beings from God. Like all beings, they are good and beautiful and forever. They came here to live and learn and laugh and grow. They are the youngest ambassadors of God.

The greatest gift you can give them is to help them remember who they are. As soon as they can grasp the concepts, teach them about their true identity and purpose and nourishment. Teach them through words and ideas and stories and games that are appropriate for each age level.

They should be taught how they share the same nature as other beings as well as how they differ a little bit. In this way, they can learn to value oneness and difference from an early age. They should also be taught that they are here on earth to represent God as his ambassadors. This is a perfect expression of their natural desire to be helpful. They can take joy in the fact that God has invited them to be his helpers.

Second, recognize that children are artists of God. They are born ready to run, play, jump, sing, dance, and paint. They see millions of colors and hear millions of sounds. The world is large and rich and diverse to them.

Whatever education they get must build on top of their natural tendencies toward this multicolored perception of the world. It should not reduce the rainbows in their eyes to just black and white. It should not reduce the symphonies in their ears to just loud and soft. It should not put the artist to sleep by turning them into little calculating machines.

They come into this world with tremendous creativity and we must not educate it right out of them. We have to help them bring forth the beauty and power of their art and contribute it to the world. The world needs their art. And they need to give their art to the world.

Third, recognize that children are students who need teachers, guides, and mentors. So guide their learning. Don't just give them the tools to learn and then walk away. Some caregivers have a tendency to teach their children very little so that they can figure it out for themselves. "Look it up," they tell them. "Find out for yourself," they tell them.

The difficulty with this approach is that there are many things that the children will never figure out until someone takes the time to teach them. How to think about God, how to pray, how to have a creative life, how to serve people, how to forgive, how to contribute to the world, how to handle failure, and so on.

Children look to your experience with these things so they can have a starting point for their own explorations. Your advice doesn't have to be a cage; it can be a map. They are not locked inside your advice. They can use it where it makes sense for them. They can change their path where it doesn't make sense. In this way, they get your best advice while also having the freedom and space to figure things out for themselves.

Fourth, teach children by example. It is not easy to be the caregiver of a child; it is actually quite difficult. It takes you out of the center of your life. You have to learn to think of the child first. But here's the interesting part that very few people talk about. The child watches you. She watches how you run your life and takes lessons from that. If you don't pay attention to your own relationship with God, the child won't either. He learns that from you. If you don't pursue your artistic life, the child won't either. The child is watching you. So you have to think of the child's development first, but that also means making your own practice a priority.

When a father values his art, the child will know to value her own. Interestingly enough, what that means is that you can't sacrifice your creative life for your child. You have to practice your art as a gift to your children, to show them that their own creative life must be pursued as a priority, especially when they have their own children.

Fifth, give children a wide education. It is not enough to teach children massive amounts of science and math and think that they are getting a proper education. Our technological society values science and math because it values controlling the physical world more than anything else. But that barely touches the wide spectrum of human experience. Children must become immersed and fluent in art, literature, religion, psychology, philosophy, history, law, politics, and many other subjects. Children aren't just little scientists and mathematicians; they are also artists, writers, teachers, counselors, healers, historians, storytellers, peacemakers, bridge builders, and public servants. Above all else, their education must include an initiation into the knowledge and wisdom that comes from remembering who they are, why they are here, and what feeds them.

Finally, let the children teach you. Every child comes into the world bearing blessings and gifts. Every one of them comes with their own unique perspective. They come to learn, of course, but they also come to teach. There might be missing pieces in your knowledge and understanding of things that they have come to fill. There might be empty and hurt places in your heart that they have come to heal. As you care for them and teach them, learn to listen to them and see the world through their eyes. They have ideas you might never have thought of and images you might never have imagined. You need the freshness of their perspective as much as they need the maturity of yours. In the miracle and magic of this mutual exchange, two beings from God can learn to recognize and delight in each other.

Work on changing your insides by learning that children are little beings from God who need our nurturing teachings. When a child is born, it is a sign that God has sent one more ambassador into the world. She is here to learn, to grow, to contribute to the work of all the ambassadors. She is here to help the world and the world is here to help her. But she can't do this on her own. She needs help. She needs caregivers, parents, grandparents, big sisters, big brothers, teachers, mentors, and allies. She needs you. You do not need to have children of your own to be in the lives of children who need you. All children need many different people to hold them in their hearts and teach them what they don't know. They need people who will not leave them alone to figure everything out by themselves. So be a teacher to the children around you. Give them what you've been given. Teach them what you've been taught. Hold them in your heart and never let them go.

DECLARE

Children are young beings from God.
I am willing to care for them and teach them.

23

CARE FOR THE EARTH

And the earth—
we have spread it out wide,
and placed firm mountains on it,
and caused life of every kind to grow on it
in a balanced manner,
and provided means of livelihood for you
as well as for all living beings
whose sustenance does not depend on you.

(Quran 15:19-20)

Have you ever been so restless and troubled that you had to get up and take a walk outside? You wanted to see the blue of the skies and the brown bark of the trees and the green blades of grass. You wanted to feel the yellow sunlight on your face. You wanted to hear the sound of red birds. You wanted to watch gray squirrels chase each other around. And for a few minutes, you found a sense of relief from whatever was bothering you. You felt like you were welcomed as a part of the earth and a member of a larger family. A quiet restoration took place inside you when you spent time outside.

It is strange that we should spend our entire physical lives on the earth and yet not think much about the earth. We know that we need food, water, and air from the earth for our bodies. We also know that we need wood, iron, and other resources to build our homes, towns, and tools. What we don't often acknowledge is that the soil, the wind, the mountains, and the rivers heal our minds and hearts. What we don't often admit is that walking in the company of trees and flowers and birds and bees gives us an immediate joy.

This forgetfulness makes us enter into a relationship with the earth that is often one-sided. We take much and give back little. Then we take too much and give back nothing. We not only use the earth as we see fit, we overuse it. We pretend to forget that if we disturb the soil, the plants can't grow. If we poison the rivers, the fish can't live. If we pollute the air, no one can breathe. We don't have a lifetime warranty on the earth. We can't return the whole planet and get a new one. We also can't abandon it and find a similar earth in another galaxy. If we want to change our relationship to the earth, we first have to change our ideas about the earth.

This verse says that God has created the earth to be a home for many living creatures. Once upon a time beyond time, God said the word "Be" and brought forth a being. He clothed that being in a physical form, but this form was not the body of a human; it was the body of a planet made out of the stuff of stars. It was hot at first and then God cooled it. He made an atmosphere around it and brought down rain. Rivers and oceans pooled on the surface. And out of the water, God made the physical form of every living thing.

The earth is a being from God. Like all beings, it is good and beautiful and forever. Like all beings, it is an ambassador of God, embodying his values and representing his interests. Since the earth is the same kind of being from God that we are, we all belong to the same family of beings. We can think of the earth as an older sister or older brother in being.

The earth is our living ancestor. Our human bodies are made from its planetary body. We eat the food of the earth. We drink the water of the earth. We breathe the air of the earth. The health of our physical lives depends on the health of the earth. The earth is not a dead piece of rock that happens to be our accidental home. It is a living organism that hosts and feeds many plants, animals, and humans. We can think of the earth as our great grandmother and great grandfather.

The earth is our teacher. God has entrusted it with the holy task of being a bearer of life and of being an environment of learning for a wide variety of living creatures. Here they can have the opportunity to be born, to learn, to grow, to explore their potentials, and to fulfill their destinies. The earth embodies the signs of God for all creatures. If we want to understand God a little better, we can study the earth like a book of God's creativity and wisdom. We can think of the earth as a school of knowledge.

If we think about the earth as a fellow being from God, as an ancestor, and a teacher, then a different picture of the earth comes into view. The earth seems more like a person who deserves our respect, rather than a thing we can exploit. Our whole way of life has regarded the earth as a lifeless thing. We now have to build a new way of life that regards the earth as a living being. That means we have to reimagine and redesign our relationship with the earth entirely.

Where do you begin? First, get to know your own body. God made your body from the earth's body, so the closest part of the earth to you is your own body. There are several core things that your body needs to be healthy: natural food, clean water, clean air, playful movement, and sound sleep. If your body doesn't get these things on a daily basis, it won't be as healthy and strong as it could be. So take good care of your body. Practice breathing slowly and deeply. Take long walks where you pay attention to every step, every sound, and every scent. Eat and chew your food slowly. Savor all your physical experiences. Give thanks to God for all the miracles that go into making your body work in all the ways that it does.

Second, get to know the earth. As your ancestor, the earth has a lot to teach you. In fact, you came to the earth to receive that wisdom from it. So spend your time looking, listening, and learning from it. The earth is a book that contains nothing less than the signs of God himself. Find nearby places where you can be alone with the earth: in a park, on a hiking trail, on the slopes of a mountain, on the banks of a river, on the shores of an ocean. Try to feel the presence of God all around you. Listen to the voice of God communicating with you through everything you see, hear, and touch.

Third, take responsibility for the earth. The more familiar you become with your own body's pleasures and pains, the more you can extend that awareness to feel the earth's own pleasures and pains. In the same way that your body becomes sick when it doesn't get good food and water, the earth becomes sick when its soil and rivers and atmosphere are polluted. This affects all the living creatures that depend on the earth to stay healthy and strong.

Whatever you do to the earth, you do to yourself. So take good care of the earth. Be mindful of how you use its resources. When you make something and share it with the world, you have to think hard about the consequences. You have to make sure it doesn't harm the earth and the growth of life. You have to make sure it doesn't lead to imbalance. You have to give back as much as you take, if not more. You have to make sure you are being helpful and not harmful, especially for future generations. So take personal responsibility for the garden God entrusted to you. After all, the earth is here not just for us, but for every creature God has created to live on it.

Finally, think about the future. If we don't adequately address the challenges we have on earth, we will infect other planets with our lack of knowledge and compassion. The last thing we need is to export our mistakes to the stars. Before we venture out into other parts of the galaxy, we have to get things right on earth first. Running away from the questions that the earth puts in front of us by running off to Mars is not the answer. Mars will ask the same questions and we still won't have any good answers. That's why we have to meet the challenges that are right in front of us today. This will require all of us to get involved and bring the best of our knowledge and compassion and creativity to the table.

Work on changing your insides by learning how to care for the earth. It is our only home. We can't keep using and abusing the earth as a raw resource as if there are no consequences. We have to learn to see the earth as a fellow being from God, as an ancestor, and as a teacher. In the same way that the earth has a responsibility toward us, we have a responsibility toward the earth. We are both ambassadors joined together on a common purpose to represent God's interests. Only by learning to work together in a mutually respectful partnership can we live on the earth in a sustainable manner for generations to come.

DECLARE

The earth is my home.
I will take care of my home.

24

STAND UP FOR JUSTICE

O you who believe!
Be guardians of justice
as witnesses for God,
even though it is against yourselves,
your parents, or your family,
whether it concerns a rich man or a poor man,
for God is nearer to both.
So don't let yourself deviate from justice.
If you distort the testimony or refuse,
then be sure that God is aware
of everything you do.

(Quran 4:135)

When you see a homeless man on the street, what do you think to yourself? When you see a rich man, wearing a nice suit, getting into his expensive car, what do you think to yourself?

Let's be honest: we probably admire the rich man because we envy his wealth. We probably look away from the poor man because we fear his poverty. One man looks clean; the other looks dirty. One man looks triumphant; the other looks defeated. So we treat the one who looks like he's winning the game better than the one who looks like he's losing. After all, we cheer the winners and walk away from the losers.

We give the rich man one kind of justice; we give the poor man a lesser kind of justice or no justice at all. We follow this pattern not only with wealth, but also with gender, skin color, nationality, ethnicity, language, and class. We want to see more people who share our privileges and look like us. We are less interested in seeing people who have none of our advantages and look different from us. So a quiet choice is always being made: rich and alike is good while poor and different is bad.

A justice that favors the rich group at the expense of every other group can't claim to be justice at all. The game is rigged. The dice are loaded. In the theater of justice, the actors may go through their motions, but the outcome has already been decided by the playwright and the director long before the performance has even started. The justice of the rich writes plays that always reward the rich and punish the poor.

This verse calls us to be guardians of justice. It calls us to watch over justice because it can be easily manipulated. We bear witness for God, even if it means admitting that we allowed the injustice to happen. When a wrong has been done by one party to another, we search for the whole truth to shed light on both parties. We don't hide some of the truth so that the rich side always wins and the poor side always loses. God is watching how well we maintain the integrity of justice.

The justice of God is not the rule of the mob. People who are enraged by whatever threats they perceive are looking not to practice justice, but to commit violence. The justice of God is not the law of the land. That is merely the justice of the privileged written out. It's what the lawmakers put down in their law books to safeguard their own interests and access to resources above and beyond everyone else. The justice of God is not the justice of "an eye for an eye." As it has been said, such a justice makes the whole world go blind. Some people believe that justice needs to be blind so that it can be applied equally to all, but we actually need a justice that can see.

The justice of God is the justice of seeing people as God sees them. Our practice of justice must be, first and foremost, a remembrance of who people really are. They are not just plaintiffs and defendants. They are beings from God who are good and beautiful and forever. They are ambassadors of God who are here on earth to represent his interests.

Disagreements have occurred. Mistakes have been made. Crimes have been committed. How can justice help them both get back on track? How can a justice that sees help them both to remember who they are and why they are here? How can it help them renew their commitment to live and work together in civility, cooperation, and community? Instead of being a punisher, could justice be a teacher?

This is why we don't need blind justice. We need a justice whose eyes are both compassionate and piercing. We need justice to take off its blindfolds and take a look around at all the people of God who have either been committing injustice or have been suffering under injustice.

The rich man is a noble creation of God who seems to have been given much wealth. The poor man is a noble creation of God who seems to have been given much less wealth. If we want to be guardians of justice, then we will have to train our eyes to see that both of these men are noble creations of God. The wealth of one of them doesn't make him more worthy of justice. The lack of wealth of the other doesn't make him less worthy of justice. God is near to both of them.

But justice should not stop here. Now that it can see, it should probe further into every injustice. Justice should ask if the rich man participates in maintaining a culture of inequality where wealth flows more and more to rich men like himself and less and less to poor men. Is this why the rich get richer and the poor get poorer? Does this one-sided advantage properly serve both of them, especially since they are both near to God and entrusted to reflect God's values on earth?

Under this injustice, how can the poor man serve God fully with all of his time, knowledge, and gifts if he is left burdened and buried underneath his poverty? How can the rich man serve God properly by sharing his wealth if he is left poisoned by his pride and greed? Neither of them can fulfill their role as ambassadors of God. This situation is unjust not only to the poor man, but also to the rich man. A justice that privileges the rich and a culture that favors the wealthy does both of them a disservice.

So how do you address and heal this injustice? First, stand up for the justice of God in how you see people. Practice seeing all people—rich and poor, black and brown and white, highly educated or less educated—as your fellow beings from God. Every single one of them deserves to live a long strong life where they can unfold their God-given potential. If they suffer injustice, it is your responsibility to defend them and help them overcome it. If they inflict injustice on others, it is your responsibility to stop them and lead them back to justice.

Second, stand up for the justice of God in every community. When a community is filled with people who don't see others as God sees them, then they create social institutions and cultural practices based on injustice. They build neighborhoods, schools, businesses, governments, shops, banks, and so on to serve one group of people better than every other group. Instead of creating equal access to opportunities and resources for all, they put them in the hands of a select few. You have to stay awake, pay attention, and speak up every time you see this happening.

To bring justice back into a community, you have to take the lead in asking the hard questions: "Who are we? Where do we want to go? What have we done? What did we miss? Does this reflect the best in us or the worst in us? Who did we include? Who did we exclude? What do we want to show? What are we trying to hide? Who are we trying to benefit? Whose benefits are we trying to take away?" This is the regular self-examination that justice requires everyone to undertake. And then you can lead your community in writing a new play for justice where everyone is seen as God sees them.

Lastly, stand up for the justice of God by joining a movement or starting one. To make any substantial change, you have to join forces with others. Standing up, speaking out, gathering support, challenging unjust social values and vicious cultural norms, passing new laws to replace old ones, imagining new words, phrases, images, icons, and stories to trigger a cultural shift: these are the tactics and artifacts of change. Awareness and prayer, hopes and dreams, can fuel a movement. But it takes a group of people working together consistently to implement a strategy persistently to make real social change. So find your allies, build your tribe, align on your methods and goals, and get to work in all the ways that honor God.

Work on changing your insides by learning that standing up for justice means building a culture where the blessing of every human being is recognized, protected, and celebrated. Woman or man, child or adult, poor or rich, sick or healthy, dark-skin or light-skin, immigrant or native-born, highly educated or less educated: God is near to them all. See people as God sees them. Serve their best interests and highest potential. Work toward a more just society where everyone is included and no one is excluded. We are each other's blessing. To stand up for justice is to be grateful for that blessing.

DECLARE

I stand up for the justice of God.
I lead my community toward the justice of God.

25

BUILD BRIDGES

Surely those who believe
and the Jews and the Christians
and the Sabians—
anyone who believes
in God and the Last Day
and does good in the world—
will have their reward
with their Lord;
they will have nothing
to fear or grieve.

(Quran 2:62)

Were you ever told that the only people who
are going to heaven are the ones who belong

to your particular religious tradition? Somehow you were lucky enough to be born into the one right religion. But everyone else, possibly billions of other people, weren't so lucky. Even though they might be moral people, they were still going to hell simply because they were not members of your religious tradition. Does that sound familiar?

How did you feel about this? Did you feel relieved that you had found the one right religion? Did you feel superior over others who were hopelessly lost? Or did you feel disturbed that your tradition would even entertain such an idea and take pleasure in it? Why would a merciful God create people, take such good care of them, and yet so easily condemn them to the pain of hell? Did you ever find that this way of thinking about God and his mercy never felt quite right?

When we claim to have special access to God that no one else can have, we are not telling the truth. We are trying to squeeze God into the shape of our fear and hatred. We are trying to trap him inside the narrowness of our own religious tradition. But God is big. He is bigger than the heavens and the earth. He is wider than all the galaxies scattered across the universe. He is more vast than our intelligence and imagination can even comprehend. In other words, God can't be limited by his creation. A god who can be shrunk down to fit inside our religious tradition is not a god, but an illusion.

When God said "Be" and brought us into being, he established a permanent relationship with each and every one of us. Every single being has their own unlimited access to God that no other being can take away. No single group of people has exclusive access to God. God is the God of all people without exception. He teaches, guides, and cares for us all. Anyone who learns what God is teaching, follows his guidance, and cares for all people and all creatures is practicing the broad religion that God has sent down in different forms.

This verse says that anyone who believes in God and does good in the world will receive God's grace, guidance, and mercy—here in this world and in the hereafter. This is a broad definition of religion that does not limit itself to a single tradition. This definition includes Jews and Christians specifically because they belong to the same family of traditions as Muslims.

Interestingly enough, this verse also mentions the Sabians. They were a people of Arabia who believed in one God. They were not Jewish or Christian. They were also not necessarily a part of the early Muslim community either. But since they were a moral people who believed in the one God, he included them in his mercy. This verse then extends God's mercy to everyone who believes and does good. This covers all moral people of all faiths: past, present, and future.

So what is the meaning of heaven, hell, and earth in light of this broader definition of religion? There are people who strive and succeed in remembering their identity and fulfilling their purpose on earth.

God increases his blessings and gifts upon them and allows them to grow in knowledge and compassion. Like a teacher promoting a successful student from one grade to the next, God promotes and advances those who closely follow his guidance. This is the meaning of heaven.

There are also those people who try to follow God's guidance, but it is quite difficult for them. They forget. They get distracted. They have good intentions, but they still have trouble practicing their relationship to God and their responsibility toward all people. They are not misguided or lost. They are simply students who need more time in the same learning environment to practice their lessons. This is the meaning of earth.

And then there are those people who not only refuse to follow God's guidance, they deliberately go against it. Whatever God says to do, they do the opposite. If he says to be kind, they are cruel. If he says to be generous, they steal from others. If he says to be forgiving, they hold grudges and take revenge. Where there is cooperation, they bring conflict. Where there is peace, they bring war. They not only make their own lives difficult, they make the lives of everyone around them difficult. But God is not going to give up on them. He's going to use more severe lessons to get through their hardened hearts. This is the meaning of hell.

In this way, heaven, hell, and earth can be seen as a place, a state of mind, as well as an experience of the hereafter. By remembering or not remembering our identity and purpose, we create our own heaven or hell right here on earth. In other words, how much you actually orient your mind and heart toward God and how much you actually care for people is more important than how you closely you follow the rituals of your religious tradition.

At the same time, each religious tradition is a valuable resource. As long as it holds God's teachings, it holds God's blessings. When people follow a tradition with knowledge and compassion, these blessings can be released and received. And whatever blessings one tradition holds never stops any other tradition from holding similar blessings and teachings from God. After all, God has created us all, spread us out over the earth, and spoke to each group in different languages using different stories to address different circumstances. Each religious tradition is a torn piece of a larger map from God.

Wouldn't it be valuable to collect all the pieces of the map together so we can get a bigger picture of what God has been teaching? Wouldn't it be useful to gather up the points of data, look for patterns, and draw out the most useful ones? We can identify which ideas occur repeatedly across the religions. And we can also identify which ideas are local to each religion, like a unique signature. In this way, we can triangulate which truths are universal for all time and which truths are particular to specific times and circumstances.

How do you begin? First, study deeply a religion that is not your own. Read its history, its philosophy, its theology, its art, and so on. You will see patterns similar to the ones in your religion. Then you will understand that religion is a common social phenomenon that follows similar patterns. Ask yourself what you have learned from this religion that helps you go deeper into your own religion. What one religion touches upon, another religion might elaborate. What one religion ignores, another religion might perform an in-depth investigation. And you can learn from all of this.

Second, inspired by your study of another religion, go back to your own religion and study it just as deeply, as if you are looking at it for the first time with new eyes. Dive into its history, philosophy, theology, artwork, and so on. Learn to ask the hard questions and offer generous answers. Share what you find with others because it will deepen your understanding even further.

Third, build bridges with people from different traditions. In the same way that we reach out to people who are different from us in order to see our common humanity, we reach out to different traditions to learn about our common values. Your particular tradition may have ideas that are quite different from their particular tradition, but what you have in common is much larger than your differences. On that commonality, build bridges of friendship and community.

Recognize them as your sisters and brothers. They are members of your family in the family of beings. They are your companions in the remembrance and service of God. Be their sister; be their brother. Open your arms and welcome them into your mind and heart. Join them in their prayer halls and services and invite them to yours. Learn about their practices and commitments and teach them about yours. You're not trying to convert each other; you're trying to share notes, swap stories, and widen each other's maps of God.

Work on changing your insides by learning that God includes in his mercy all who believe in him and do good. He has revealed himself in many different ways to many different religious traditions. Each one contains valuable truths for all of us. We have to study his signs as they show up in each tradition. Only in this way can our understanding of God stretch across multiple traditions, instead of being limited to our particular tradition. Only in this way can we appreciate that we are all in this together: making maps, telling stories, sharing notes, and walking hand in hand inside the vastness of the beauty and mystery of God.

DECLARE

I build bridges across religions.
Every religion helps me go deeper into my own.

2 6

DON'T BE AFRAID

Don't be afraid;
surely God is with us.

(Quran 9:40)

What are you afraid of? What scares you the most? What makes you feel that you are all alone? What makes you feel powerless? As you look back over your life, can you point out moments when you made certain decisions only because you were scared?

Fear. It might be the hardest topic for any of us to talk about. We are so eager to show each other the highlights of our lives, our bravest days, our greatest accomplishments, and our most joyful experiences. And yet we hesitate at best and we hide at worst our fears, struggles, and failures. Some people think that being afraid is the same thing as being weak. And who would want to show the world how weak you might be? So we hide our fears like we hide our weaknesses.

Fear is the thing that makes us look away when we look too long into our own eyes in the mirror. Fear convinces us to keep sitting when we begin to entertain the idea of standing up. Fear compels us to keep quiet when we have something we need to say. Fear warns us not to rock the boat even when we know how to swim. Fear draws our attention to our comfortable life when we start to imagine a more meaningful and adventurous life. Fear tells us that nothing we do matters when God teaches us that everything we do matters.

This verse reminds us to not be afraid because God is with us. There is an interesting relationship between God and fear in our lives. If we have a great deal of fear, then we will also notice that we have not yet invited God into the picture at all. If we have a strong sense of God, then any lingering fear remains small. God and fear can't both dominate our minds and hearts at the same level of intensity. The one we choose to focus on gets stronger and takes over.

"Don't be afraid" doesn't mean don't have any fears. We are going to have fears. They will cross our minds. They are thoughts of what unpleasant or unwanted things might happen. We don't have to entertain these thoughts. We don't have to put our hearts into them. And we certainly don't have to look to our fears to teach us who we are and how we are going to act in any situation.

"God is with us" means focus on God, not on the fear. We are not alone with our fears. Our creator, our teacher, and our friend is with us. We look to God to teach us who we are and how we will act. Instead of being intensely aware of the feeling of fear, we are going to be intensely aware of the teaching presence of God. God is not going to make the fear go away immediately. He's going to help us look at the fear courageously and unmask it. He's going to help us go through it by outgrowing it.

Fear is not an enemy we need to fight, but a messenger who has come with a message for us. Our fear has come to show us what areas of our understanding are too small. It comes to show us where we are not relying on God enough. If we are scared and we bring God into the picture, then we can let the sense of our fear and the sense of God dwell together. We can ask God to look at the fear with us. This is where things get interesting. We may not understand why we are scared, but God does. He can look at the fear with us and give us the gift of his perspective.

If we spend time looking at our fear with God, we will notice that, next to God, our fear is not as big as it once seemed. Anything we try to hide or cover up will seem bigger and more powerful to us than anything else. If we are unwilling to look at it, then we are saying that it has power over us and the very sight of it might destroy us, so we are going to hide it and avoid it. And this avoidance is what paralyzes us and stops us from facing the fear and going through it.

So how do you actually deal with fear as it comes up? First, remember who you are and the One who made you. You have to step out of who you think you are and more firmly into who God knows you to be. Fear is drawn to mistaken identities. If you want to overcome fear, stop being mistaken about your identity.

Remember that you are a being from God. You are not limited to your body and its fragilities. You are not limited to your mind and its blindspots. And you are certainly not limited to your heart and its resistances. You may *feel* frightened by fear, but you can't *be* frightened by fear. Why? Fear can make your body sweat, your mind freeze, and your heart tremble, but it has no effect on the being that you are. No fear will ever destroy you because God made you to never be destroyed. He made the being that you are to live and thrive forever. In your remembrance of that lives your ability to handle fear with courage and grace.

Second, commit to the truth that lives behind all fears. A fear will try to cover up the truth, like a dark cloud covers up the sun. A fear may also masquerade as the truth. That's how you know it's not the truth, but an illusion. Anything that claims to be the truth and yet doesn't foster a goodness and beauty that lasts forever is not the truth at all, but a lie. The feeling of fear is an alert that we have mistaken lies for the truth.

So when you are afraid, ask yourself: "What is the truth in this situation? And what is the lie?" Then you will gradually learn that when you are afraid, you have bought into a lie. The truth will never make you feel afraid. It will only make you feel blessed, thankful, kind, generous, forgiving, strong, brave, and true. After all, the being that you are is the truth of who you are. The more you get centered in that, the less you can be influenced by any fear.

And lastly, choose courage over fear. Fear will make you doubt if God really cares about you. It will make you doubt if caring about other people is really worth the trouble. It will make you doubt if there is anything good and beautiful in you. It will make you avoid assuming full responsibility for your role on earth as an ambassador and artist of God.

Fear will not make you do any of this in a sudden dramatic way. It will do it slowly, quietly, and gradually. Before you know it, you are living a life much smaller than what God had intended for you. And isn't that what fear does? Fear shrinks life. But life can never be shrunk; only your perception and understanding of it can.

When fear tries to make you live inside its small narrow box, have courage and reach for the God who has given you vast open spaces that stretch out wider than the heavens and the earth. Invite God to stand with you in the face of your fear. Then you can meet your fear with curiosity and understanding, rather than shock and panic and helplessness and despair. Then you can open your fear like a door and go through it and receive whatever blessing and insight it came to give you.

Once you realize that the fear was reminding you that you had forgotten who you are, then you can choose to remember. Once you realize that the fear was showing you what areas in your understanding needed to include God, then you can choose to invite God into those areas. This changes and expands your mind and heart, and that changes and expands your insides. You are no longer the exact same person you were when the fear found you. You've outgrown that person so the fear has outlived its usefulness. The fear can now dissolve and disappear because it is no longer needed.

Work on changing your insides by learning that there is no need for you to be afraid because God is always with you. You are not trying to pretend that you don't feel fear. What you are doing is focusing more on God and less on the fear. You are not letting the fear make your decisions for you. It should not color your perception and understanding. It should not silence you when you want to speak up. It should not keep the door closed when you want to open it. Only your courageous service and devotion to God should make your decisions for you. Fear might show up from time to time and offer to keep you warm, but you can refuse to wear it. God has already clothed you in courage—and courage looks good on you.

DECLARE

I will not be afraid.
God is with me.

2 7

TAKE MUHAMMAD AS AN EXAMPLE

Surely in the messenger of God
you have a good example
for him who looks to God and the Last Day,
and remembers God much.

(Quran 33:21)

Did you ever have a favorite teacher? Did she bring life and personality to what she taught so that even a boring subject could become exciting in her hands?

Did you ever have a mentor who you could go to for all kinds of questions? Even if he couldn't help you find satisfying answers, did he at least sit with you and share his experiences?

Did you ever admire an artist who inspired you to work on your own art? Did you find yourself being influenced by her style so much that you remixed some of the elements of her art into yours?

All these teachers, mentors, and artists accelerate our ability to learn. By ourselves, we can only go so far. By studying others and studying with others, however, we can make substantial progress in our practice. We can learn to do something well by letting someone else show us how they have been doing it well. This is why students study with teachers, why athletes practice with coaches, and why artists apprentice themselves to a master artist. Studying with an expert speeds up our ability to pick it up.

This verse says that we have a good example in the Prophet Muhammad (peace be upon him) of the kind of person God wants us to be. We can look to him as a teacher who brings life and personality to the principles of the Quran. We can see him as a mentor who shares his valuable experiences with us. We can regard him as an artist who inspires us with hints and clues to make art out of our own daily lives. Let's take a closer look at a few examples from his life to see what we can learn from him.

First of all, Prophet Muhammad was an orphan. This made it difficult for him to feel like he belonged anywhere. Even though he was raised by his uncle, he didn't feel connected to the larger community in Mecca. When he grew older, he used to take time away from his family and work so he could sit in a cave to think and pray and reflect. He was searching for a sense of belonging by communing with his creator and contemplating all of creation.

What can you learn from this? Even though you may have been born into a difficult situation, the being that you are can rise above it. You can take time to develop your relationship with God. You can unfold and explore your gifts as an artist of God. You can remember God and study his signs throughout creation. In this way, you can learn that you belong to God and all of creation.

Second, Prophet Muhammad lived an honorable life. He was called the sincere one because he was always honest and fair in his business dealings. In a time when women were considered the property of men, he worked for an independent business woman named Khadija. They later married and had a daughter named Fatima, who was the apple of his eye. He worked hard to raise the status of women in his society.

What can you learn from this? No matter what you see other people doing, you can always be kind and generous and honest and hard-working. You can acknowledge women and men as equals. All women deserve everything all men have enjoyed for thousands of years. Work hard to build a society where women and men live with equal rights, resources, and opportunities.

Third, when Prophet Muhammad first started sharing his message in Mecca, he was insulted and ridiculed, but he kept on sharing the message without insulting anyone back. He affirmed that the

God who had sent Adam, Noah, Abraham, Moses, David, Solomon, Joseph, and Jesus as messengers to their own people had also sent him.

What can you learn from this? As you begin to share your gifts with the world as the ambassador and artist of God, some people will criticize you and ridicule you. Don't let that stop you or distract you. You have to keep sharing your gifts. You have to keep being kind and generous and civil. All the prophets were ridiculed for the work they did on God's behalf. They kept going, so you keep going.

Finally, Prophet Muhammad always put God first. No matter what he was saying or thinking or doing, he brought God into the picture again and again. No matter how many people followed him and no matter how much his influence spread, he always regarded himself as a humble servant of God. He never put a crown on his head.

What can you learn from this? Put God first. Begin everything you do in the name of God. Finish everything you do by giving thanks to God. You can achieve many things in life, but none of them are due to you. They are always due to the grace and mercy of God. You can always stay humble and grateful for that.

These are just a few of the details of Prophet Muhammad's life. They offer us good examples of the principles he practiced. They give us food for thought on how we can put these principles into practice in our own lives. For example, when some-one hurts us, we could ask ourselves, "What did the

Prophet Muhammad do when someone hurt him?" When we have a choice to make between right and wrong in our business dealings, we could ask ourselves, "How did the Prophet Muhammad conduct his business life?" When we feel stuck and can't seem to figure out what to do next, we could ask ourselves, "What did the Prophet Muhammad do when he needed some advice or support?" In this way, we can draw inspiration from the Prophet's words and deeds.

Not only is he a teacher and a mentor, he is also an artist who teaches us about the art of life. For example, when an art teacher gets up in front of the class and draws a bowl of fruit on the board, we have to try to draw the same thing along with him because at this early stage we are just starting to learn the techniques. Once we are familiar with those techniques, we can experiment with the colors, shapes, perspectives, and textures far beyond anything we were taught in that first class. We don't have to make our fruit look like our teacher's fruit. In fact, if we get stuck on our teacher's example, we will miss the principle behind the example. But if we are able to draw out and understand the principle, we will be able to apply it to many different circumstances.

In the same way, the life and teachings of the Prophet Muhammad are a good example for us. It doesn't mean that we have to imitate the Prophet exactly. He was a seventh-century Arab prophet and businessman. His way of thinking, feeling, speaking, and acting were tied to his time and place. We are different people living in different circumstances, so we can't copy him exactly. We have to draw out the principles behind his words and deeds, reimagine them for our own time and place, and embody them through our own unique thoughts, feelings, and actions. In other words, to follow the example of the Prophet Muhammad is not to imitate his biography, but to creatively adapt his principles into our unique lives.

Even though the Prophet passed away physically from this earth over 1300 years ago, he is still very much with us. Like Moses and Jesus, his work as a prophet of God doesn't end just because his physical life came to an end. The beings that we are and the being that he is are all joined together in the family of beings. Our bond with him, like our bond with each other, is forever. His presence continues to bless us and teach us as we continue to bless him and learn from him. We affirm our relationship with him whenever we send blessings upon him, while thinking of him or saying his name: "May the peace and blessings of God be upon him."

Work on changing your insides by learning that the Prophet Muhammad left us a lifetime of examples on how to be devoted servants of God. Some people think he was an ordinary man. Like all men, he was born, lived on this earth for a number of years, and died. But there is nothing ordinary about a man who responds fully when God calls him. His life was not easy, and yet he stood up in it as a man of God. He didn't let the difficulties of his day distract him from his devotion to God. He remembered who he is and why he is here. He searched for the God who made him and brought back the Quran. He cleared a new path for us and showed us a better way. He reset our relationship with God by teaching us that God is caring and compassionate, that the earth is a beautiful garden, and that we are all blessed. Give thanks to God for sending the Prophet Muhammad. He has truly been a mercy upon us all.

DECLARE

I study the example of Prophet Muhammad.
I follow the principles behind his practice.

EPILOGUE

28

BE GOD'S HELPERS

O you who believe! Be God's helpers.

(Quran 61:14)

Have you ever watched small children interact with each other in a classroom? Each child is usually doing what they want to do out of their own self-interest. But there comes a moment when the teacher asks, "Who will help me pick up the crayons and put the toys away?" Many little hands rise up in the air and the children declare with excitement, "Me! Me! Me!" They suddenly find themselves being called and drawn to a larger purpose as the teacher's helpers. Then they follow the teacher's guidance and put away all the crayons and toys.

This small gesture, no matter how brief it is, con-nects them to the teacher, the classroom, and each other. It makes them feel like they belong, that they have a role to play, and that they can make contributions with their own minds and hearts and hands. All this mirrors our own relationship to God in which he is our teacher, creation is the classroom, and we are his students.

This verse calls us to be God's helpers. When God said "Be" and brought us into being, he made us his words. He made us a part of his own language. We are the words he uses to tell the story of creation. When God wants something to be done, he sends us to make it happen by his command and on his behalf. We are the words he speaks over his creation, like a blessing, an incantation, or an enchantment. When we respond fully to God's call to be his helpers, we help him unfold and extend the story of creation in new, creative, and powerful directions.

God is the storytelling creator who wants to hear new stories from his storytelling creatures. The whole universe is making and telling stories. You yourself have many stories to tell. You can tell new stories that change past stories. You can change a life by telling a better story. You can bend the direction of creation toward remembrance, justice, knowledge, and compassion by the power of your story.

So don't take the blessing of being God's word and all your inner and outer gifts for granted and do very little with them. Use the word that you are to tell new stories. Be helpful. Lend a hand. Share your blessings. Give your gifts. Contribute something. Offer some assistance. God is working in the world. He's helping everyone and telling them new stories. Won't you be a part of his story? Won't you help someone today with their story?

There are many people who live and suffer inside their small stories. They think that the rough life they were born into or the harsh circumstances that surround them is the only thing they will ever experience in the world. They don't have the knowledge or the means to outgrow their rough life or overcome their harsh circumstances. The story of their life, the story they keep repeating to themselves, remains small and hopeless.

The God of infinite possibilities, however, has no desire to see any of his people trapped in such finite lives. This is where you come in. When God calls you to be his helper, he is calling you to help them tell a new story, a better story, a kinder story, a more generous story. You are not there to set them free. They will set themselves free by the strength of God. You will simply be a friendly reminder of their own possibilities and a sign of hope. You are there to help them remember who they are. You are there to remind them that each and every one of them is a being from God, good and beautiful and forever. By his grace and mercy and help, they will overcome and break free from their small stories and learn to tell larger and more hopeful stories.

So how do you get started in being God's helper? First of all, you make a personal decision to use your time on earth to be a helper. You are not going to sit on the sidewalk and watch the movement or the march or the protest go by. You are deciding to be a part of it. You are not an outsider; you are an insider. You are not going to hope that somebody else will do their part so you don't have to do your part. You know in your heart that if you don't get personally involved, certain things that should happen will not happen. You play a key role in all of it, so you are not going to sit this one out.

Second, you take a good hard look at God's world through his interests and values. You see what's actually going on and what kind of help is needed. You open your eyes and wake up. You don't avoid or turn away from the pain and suffering and injustices of the world. You get specific about exactly where the most help is needed. You join forces with your fellow helpers. You find your tribe or build a new one. You gather momentum. You make a difference. You change the course of events. You make God's work in the world your work in the world.

Third, you take a good look at your own blessings and gifts and skills and talents and resources—and you decide to use them. No matter who might have more skills and resources than you, God is still waiting for you to use your unique gifts to help him. Every rose gets to share its red with the world. You don't wait for the perfect time, the perfect opportunities, the perfect funding, the perfect team, the perfect tools, and the perfectly guaranteed outcome. You start right where you are with what you have.

Fourth, you start helping somebody so they get help from you before the sun goes down that day. You start so somebody can eat good food that day, drink some clean water that day, get some good advice that day, and get a door opened for them that day. And then you do it again tomorrow and the day after that and the day after that. What you're trying to do is to help someone feel more hopeful and less hopeless every single day. This is God's work.

Finally, you put yourself in a state where you are always listening for God's call and responding to it. God once called you and said "Be," and you responded by coming into being. So when God calls you again and says "Be my helper," respond by becoming his helper and helping every way you can. Now God doesn't say "Be my helper" once or twice, here and there. He is always saying "Be my helper" and always calling you to him.

The best way to respond to him is to say, "Here I am, God; at your service, here I am" (Arabic: *labbayk allahuma labbayk*). What this means is: "Here I am, I am making myself available. I am not going to hide from you anymore. I am not going to ignore you anymore. Here I am, I will be who you made me to be. I will give what you gave me to give. I will strive. I will contribute. I will make a difference. Here I am, I am willing to do it. I am happy to do it. Here I am, I am ready to serve. I am ready to help. How can I serve? How can I help?"

When you decide to be God's helper and you put yourself into this state of "Here I am," God puts you in alignment with his will and strengthens you. He puts you in a heightened state of feeling his presence all around you so you can receive his instruction and guidance. You deliberately avoid indulging in anything that would slow down or fog up your mind and heart. This reduces your need to turn to mental distractions, emotional preoccupations, or food and drink to medicate yourself from the stress and anxiety of life. You can then allow yourself to always be pulled toward God, like iron toward a magnet. This is a state where nothing influences you more than your relationship and communication with God. This helps you to stay ready to receive his call and ready to respond to it. Then you begin to understand that working as one of God's helpers on earth is nothing less than training and preparation to eventually become one of God's angels.

Work on changing your insides by learning that God is always calling you to be his helper. You are not here to save anyone. You are not here to fix the world. You are here to bless the world, listen to the world, hold hands with the world, build homes for the world, plant seeds for the world, cook food for the world, sew clothes for the world, speak up for the world, write new stories for the world, and make good art for the world. And in that holy space that you hold open, people can more easily receive the blessing and healing that God is always pouring on them. You save no one. You fix nothing. You simply become a helpful reminder. Then people remember and return to the truth of who they really are.

DECLARE

Here I am, God;
at your service, here I am.

Conclusion: The Practice of Lions

A lion who was raised by sheep has to make a sustained effort at remembering his own lion nature before it becomes natural to him once again. In the meantime, he easily falls back into the habits of thinking and feeling and acting like a sheep. To overcome his old sheep habits, he has to replace them with new lion habits—not just daily, but hourly.

We find ourselves in a similar situation. We read a lot of books. We hear a lot of things. We are exposed to a lot of ideas. But being exposed to ideas is not enough. Those ideas have to turn into food and go into our mouths and into our bodies. They have to get into our bones and blood, our minds and hearts, and come out in our actions if they're going to be useful to us and useful to the world.

Sometimes we don't know how to do this. Sometimes we can't see ourselves doing those things. It seems too hard or too foreign to us. Sometimes we think we are not the people who do those things. Doing those things would make us different kinds of people. It might change us too much. We would become strangers to ourselves.

Sometimes it frightens us to know what's on the other side of the door. We'll sit down right in front of it. We'll build a campfire and cook marshmallows and sing songs right in front of the door, but we won't go through the door. We'll caress the knob and write letters of longing to the person on the other side, but we won't go through the door. We'll dream and yearn for what might be on the other side of the door, but we will not actually open the door and walk through it. Does any of this sound familiar?

I want to invite you to use this book to finally walk through that door. The 28 verses in this book, rooted in the language and vision of the Quran, represent the core of a universal spirituality. They point out a direct path to the truth of who you are, who we are, and who God is.

These verses range from recognizing yourself as a being from God, welcoming God as your teacher and friend, embracing all people as your family, making creative contributions to your community as God's artist, standing up for justice, caring for the earth, and working for the equality of women as God's ambassador.

There is no separation here between the inner and the outer or the personal and the political or the spiritual and the worldly. It is all brightly woven in a seamless unity. If you want to grow in the fullness of who you are as a human being, then you have to practice the full range of these verses.

Start by picking one verse that is particularly meaningful to you. Read it slowly. Study the teachings. Practice the examples. Then pick another one and do the same thing. Then pick another one and another. If you're not sure you're practicing these verses properly, don't worry. Do whatever you can, and then next time go deeper. There is no perfect; there is only practice.

If you want these verses to guide you in your daily life, practice them on an hourly basis. Daily practice is hourly practice. Only with this kind of regular practice can the lion in you remember your lion nature.

Every hour, on top of the hour, remind yourself: "I am a being from God. I am good and beautiful. I am forever. I came here to share my blessings and give my gifts. I came here to serve and help. How can I serve? How can I help?"

It is quite normal that you will forget to do this. You will get distracted. You will get preoccupied and overwhelmed with the demands of your day. Don't worry. Come back to this practice at the top of the next hour. Forgot again? Try again in the next hour. Forgot again? Try again. Forgot once again? Try once again. Keep striving every single hour to remember who you are and the One who made you. Let this remembrance guide your thoughts, feelings, actions, and decisions.

This is the practice of lions: to remember your true identity inside this game of illusions, to fulfill your true purpose inside this game of distractions, and to receive your true nourishment inside this game of addictions.

You are a being from God. You are an ambassador of God. You are a student of God. You are an artist of God. You are a helper of God. Remember who you are and act accordingly.

I honor you and every effort you make on God's behalf. May the peace and blessings of God rain down on you and your family.

Ameen.
Amen.
So be it.

Rahim

The 28 Verses in their Arabic-English Forms

I have translated these 28 verses from the Quran into simple readable English, instead of trying to achieve an awkward word-for-word match between the Arabic and the English. The main goal has been to show the clear and practical meaning of each verse as well as its poetic and philosophical depths.

1. Change Your Insides

Quran 13:11

إِنَّ اللَّهَ لَا يُغَيِّرُ مَا بِقَوْمٍ حَتَّىٰ يُغَيِّرُوا مَا بِأَنْفُسِهِمْ

God doesn't change what's happening in people's lives until they first change what's happening inside themselves.

2. You are a Being from God

Quran 3:47

إِذَا قَضَىٰ أَمْرًا فَإِنَّمَا يَقُولُ لَهُ كُن فَيَكُونُ

When he decides to bring something into being, he says to it, "Be" and it is.

3. You are Good and Beautiful

Quran 32:7

الَّذِي أَحْسَنَ كُلَّ شَيْءٍ خَلَقَهُ

He has made everyone and everything out of beautiful goodness.

4. You are Forever

Quran 2:156

إِنَّا اللهِ وَإِنَّا إِلَيْهِ رَاجِعُونَ

We belong to God and we are returning to him.

5. We are One

Quran 7:189

هُوَ الَّذِي خَلَقَكُم مِّن نَّفْسٍ وَاحِدَةٍ

He has made you all out of a single being.

6. We are Different

Quran 49:13

يَا أَيُّهَا النَّاسُ إِنَّا خَلَقْنَاكُم مِّن ذَكَرٍ وَأُنثَىٰ
وَجَعَلْنَاكُمْ شُعُوبًا وَقَبَائِلَ لِتَعَارَفُوا

O humanity! Surely, we have created you male and female and have
made you nations and tribes so you might know one another.

7. We are Ambassadors

Quran 6:165

وَهُوَ الَّذِي جَعَلَكُمْ خَلَائِفَ الْأَرْضِ

He has made you all ambassadors on the earth.

8. God is One

Quran 47:19

لَا إِلَهَ إِلَّا اللَّهُ

There is no god but God.

9. God is a Teacher

Quran 96:1-5

اقْرَأْ بِاسْمِ رَبِّكَ الَّذِي خَلَقَ
خَلَقَ الْإِنسَانَ مِنْ عَلَقٍ
اقْرَأْ وَرَبُّكَ الْأَكْرَمُ
الَّذِي عَلَّمَ بِالْقَلَمِ
عَلَّمَ الْإِنسَانَ مَا لَمْ يَعْلَمْ

Recite! in the name of your Lord who created, created you all from a clot. Recite! and your Lord is the most Generous, who taught by the pen, taught you all what you did not know.

10. God is a Friend

Quran 2:257

اللَّهُ وَلِيُّ الَّذِينَ آمَنُوا

God is the friend of those who believe.

11. Remember God

Quran 13:28

أَلَا بِذِكْرِ اللَّهِ تَطْمَئِنُّ الْقُلُوبُ

Surely in the remembrance of God do hearts find peace.

12. Give Thanks to God

Quran 31:12

اشْكُرْ لِلَّهِ ۚ وَمَن يَشْكُرْ فَإِنَّمَا يَشْكُرُ لِنَفْسِهِ

Give thanks to God. Those who give thanks, give thanks for their own benefit.

13. Study God's Signs

Quran 2:164

إِنَّ فِي خَلْقِ السَّمَاوَاتِ وَالْأَرْضِ وَاخْتِلَافِ اللَّيْلِ وَالنَّهَارِ وَالْفُلْكِ الَّتِي
تَجْرِي فِي الْبَحْرِ بِمَا يَنفَعُ النَّاسَ وَمَا أَنزَلَ اللَّهُ مِنَ السَّمَاءِ مِن مَّاءٍ
فَأَحْيَا بِهِ الْأَرْضَ بَعْدَ مَوْتِهَا وَبَثَّ فِيهَا مِن كُلِّ دَابَّةٍ وَتَصْرِيفِ الرِّيَاحِ
وَالسَّحَابِ الْمُسَخَّرِ بَيْنَ السَّمَاءِ وَالْأَرْضِ لَآيَاتٍ لِقَوْمٍ يَعْقِلُونَ

Surely, in the creation of the heavens and the earth, and the difference of night and day, and the ships running upon the sea, and the rain God sends down from the sky, reviving the earth after its death, and the spreading of all kinds of creatures, and the winds and the clouds between heaven and earth: these are all signs of God for a people who think.

14. Be Kind

Quran 4:36

وَبِالْوَالِدَيْنِ إِحْسَانًا وَبِذِي الْقُرْبَىٰ وَالْيَتَامَىٰ وَالْمَسَاكِينِ وَالْجَارِ ذِي
الْقُرْبَىٰ وَالْجَارِ الْجُنُبِ وَالصَّاحِبِ بِالْجَنبِ وَابْنِ السَّبِيلِ وَمَا مَلَكَتْ

أَيْمَانُكُمْ إِنَّ اللَّهَ لَا يُحِبُّ مَن كَانَ مُخْتَالًا فَخُورًا

Be kind to your parents and family, and to the orphans and the needy, and to neighbors and travelers and servants. Surely, God doesn't love those who are proud and boastful.

15. Be Generous

Quran 2:274

الَّذِينَ يُنفِقُونَ أَمْوَالَهُم بِاللَّيْلِ وَالنَّهَارِ سِرًّا وَعَلَانِيَةً فَلَهُمْ أَجْرُهُمْ عِندَ رَبِّهِمْ وَلَا خَوْفٌ عَلَيْهِمْ وَلَا هُمْ يَحْزَنُونَ

Those who share their wealth by night and day, privately and publicly, surely their reward is with their Lord. They will have nothing to fear or grieve.

16. Be Patient and Forgiving

Quran 42:43

وَلَمَن صَبَرَ وَغَفَرَ إِنَّ ذَلِكَ لَمِنْ عَزْمِ الْأُمُورِ

And whoever is patient and forgives: that is surely the most noble thing to do.

17. Be a Student

Quran 20:114

قُل رَّبِّ زِدْنِي عِلْمًا

Say: "My Lord, increase me in knowledge."

18. Be an Artist

Quran 31:20

أَلَمْ تَرَوْا أَنَّ اللَّهَ سَخَّرَ لَكُم مَّا فِي السَّمَاوَاتِ وَمَا فِي الْأَرْضِ وَأَسْبَغَ
عَلَيْكُمْ نِعَمَهُ ظَاهِرَةً وَبَاطِنَةً

Don't you see that God has given you every single thing in the heavens and the earth, and has made you abundant with inner and outer gifts?

19. Be a Partner

Quran 78:8

وَخَلَقْنَاكُمْ أَزْوَاجًا

And we created you in pairs.

20. Honor Your Parents

Quran 17:23-24

وَقَضَىٰ رَبُّكَ أَلَّا تَعْبُدُوا إِلَّا إِيَّاهُ وَبِالْوَالِدَيْنِ إِحْسَانًا ۚ إِمَّا يَبْلُغَنَّ عِندَكَ
الْكِبَرَ أَحَدُهُمَا أَوْ كِلَاهُمَا فَلَا تَقُل لَّهُمَا أُفٍّ وَلَا تَنْهَرْهُمَا وَقُل لَّهُمَا قَوْلًا
كَرِيمًا

وَاخْفِضْ لَهُمَا جَنَاحَ الذُّلِّ مِنَ الرَّحْمَةِ وَقُل رَّبِّ ارْحَمْهُمَا كَمَا رَبَّيَانِي
صَغِيرًا

Your Lord has commanded that you worship no one except him, and that you show kindness to your parents. Once they reach old age, don't be irritated with them and don't criticize them, but speak to them with words of respect and grace. And pray for them by saying: "My Lord, have mercy on them and care for them as they cared for me when I was little."

21. Serve All Women

Quran 4:1

يَا أَيُّهَا النَّاسُ اتَّقُوا رَبَّكُمُ الَّذِي خَلَقَكُم مِّن نَّفْسٍ وَاحِدَةٍ وَخَلَقَ مِنْهَا زَوْجَهَا وَبَثَّ مِنْهُمَا رِجَالًا كَثِيرًا وَنِسَاءً وَاتَّقُوا اللَّهَ الَّذِي تَسَاءَلُونَ بِهِ وَالْأَرْحَامَ إِنَّ اللَّهَ كَانَ عَلَيْكُمْ رَقِيبًا

O people! Be careful of your duty to your Lord who created you from a single being and from it created its partner and from those two has created a multitude of women and men. Be careful of your duty toward God when you make claims of one another, and toward the wombs that gave birth to you. Surely, God is watching you.

22. Teach the Children

Quran 31:17

يَا بُنَيَّ أَقِمِ الصَّلَاةَ وَأْمُرْ بِالْمَعْرُوفِ وَانْهَ عَنِ الْمُنْكَرِ وَاصْبِرْ عَلَىٰ مَا أَصَابَكَ إِنَّ ذَلِكَ مِنْ عَزْمِ الْأُمُورِ

[The Prophet Luqman says:] O my dear son! Pray regularly and enjoin what is good and forbid what is not good, and persevere no matter what happens to you: that is surely the most noble thing to do.

23. Care for the Earth

Quran 15:19-20

وَالْأَرْضَ مَدَدْنَاهَا وَأَلْقَيْنَا فِيهَا رَوَاسِيَ وَأَنبَتْنَا فِيهَا مِن كُلِّ شَيْءٍ مَّوْزُونٍ

وَجَعَلْنَا لَكُمْ فِيهَا مَعَايِشَ وَمَن لَّسْتُمْ لَهُ بِرَازِقِينَ

And the earth—we have spread it out wide, and placed firm mountains on it, and caused life of every kind to grow on it in a balanced

manner, and provided means of livelihood for you as well as for all living beings whose sustenance does not depend on you.

24. Stand up for Justice

Quran 4:135

يَا أَيُّهَا الَّذِينَ آمَنُوا كُونُوا قَوَّامِينَ بِالْقِسْطِ شُهَدَاءَ اللَّهِ وَلَوْ عَلَىٰ أَنفُسِكُمْ أَوِ الْوَالِدَيْنِ وَالْأَقْرَبِينَ ۚ إِن يَكُنْ غَنِيًّا أَوْ فَقِيرًا فَاللَّهُ أَوْلَىٰ بِهِمَا ۖ فَلَا تَتَّبِعُوا الْهَوَىٰ أَن تَعْدِلُوا ۚ وَإِن تَلْوُوا أَوْ تُعْرِضُوا فَإِنَّ اللَّهَ كَانَ بِمَا تَعْمَلُونَ خَبِيرًا

O you who believe! Be guardians of justice as witnesses for God, even though it is against yourselves, your parents, or your family, whether it concerns a rich man or a poor man, for God is nearer to both. So don't let yourself deviate from justice. If you distort the testimony or refuse, then be sure that God is aware of everything you do.

25. Build Bridges

Quran 2:62

إِنَّ الَّذِينَ آمَنُوا وَالَّذِينَ هَادُوا وَالنَّصَارَىٰ وَالصَّابِئِينَ مَنْ آمَنَ بِاللَّهِ وَالْيَوْمِ الْآخِرِ وَعَمِلَ صَالِحًا فَلَهُمْ أَجْرُهُمْ عِندَ رَبِّهِمْ وَلَا خَوْفٌ عَلَيْهِمْ وَلَا هُمْ يَحْزَنُونَ

Surely those who believe and the Jews and the Christians and the Sabians—anyone who believes in God and the Last Day and does good in the world—will have their reward with their Lord; they will have nothing to fear or grieve.

26. Don't Be Afraid

Quran 9:40

لَا تَحْزَنْ إِنَّ اللَّهَ مَعَنَا

Don't be afraid; surely God is with us.

27. Take Muhammad as an Example

Quran 33:21

لَّقَدْ كَانَ لَكُمْ فِي رَسُولِ اللَّهِ أُسْوَةٌ حَسَنَةٌ لِّمَن كَانَ يَرْجُو اللَّهَ وَالْيَوْمَ
الْآخِرَ وَذَكَرَ اللَّهَ كَثِيرًا

Surely in the messenger of God you have a good example for him who looks to God and the Last Day, and remembers God much.

28. Be God's Helpers

Quran 61:14

يَا أَيُّهَا الَّذِينَ آمَنُوا كُونُوا أَنصَارَ اللَّهِ

O you who believe! Be God's helpers.

ABOUT RAHIM SNOW

Rahim Snow has been studying religion, spirituality, mythology, and psychology for over 30 years.

He pursued Islamic Studies at the graduate level in London before completing his Master's degree in Religion from the University of Oxford.

His main interest is in digging out the hidden treasures of Islam, cross-referencing them with other religions, and sharing his findings in a practical, friendly, and creative manner.

ABOUT REMEMBRANCE STUDIO

Remembrance Studio is the research, publishing, teaching, and media company of Rahim Snow. Our mission is:

"To help the people of God remember that they are the people of God."

Through books, ebooks, video, audio, apps, courses, and workshops, we intend to share the wisdom of Islam and other religions to feed you on your own journey.

Join our mailing list at

http://join.rahimsnow.com

to read other writings

and get sneak peeks into future books

and other offerings.

REMEMBRANCE STUDIO · RAHIM SNOW ·

كن

CPSIA information can be obtained
at www.ICGtesting.com
Printed in the USA
BVOW10*1422160717

489262BV00002B/6/P